MEMORIES OF A JEWISH GIRL FROM BROOKLYN

HELENE MEISNER OELERICH

ISBN: 978-1-64314-279-1 (Paperback)
         978-1-64314-280-7 (Hardback)
         978-1-64314-327-9 (E-book)

AuthorsPress
California, USA
www.authorspress.com

Contents

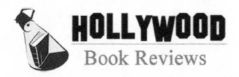

HOLLYWOOD
Book Reviews

REVIEW

BOOK TITLE: **MEMORIES OF A JEWISH GIRL FROM BROOKLYN**
AUTHOR: **HELENE MEISNER OELERICH**

REVIEWED BY: Liz Konkel

Helene Meisner Oelerich opens up about her life and experiences with all the blessings and craziness that consist of several memories which have made her who she is. She reflects on her childhood, thinking back to how her parents and her brother impacted her life, shaping her as a child that was always watching her family's actions. She delves into her relationships through various fun and wild stories which are funny, embarrassing, and even jaw-dropping. She looks back at her friendship with Laura, her relationship with Johnny Carson, her marriages, her amazing son, and her dreams.

The memoir has a reflective and conversational tone as Oelerich weaves through various memories from her life which she shares as she bears her soul for all to read. Her voice is genuine and sincere which allows you to form a real connection with her and to have fun with her memories right along with her. She reflects on her childhood and through these reflections, she looks back on several poignant moments that have stood out. She successfully captures the innocence and wonder of childhood through her observations she gathered watching her parents which are lovely moments that range from watching her mom put on make-up to her dad shaving. The relationship she has with each of them is depicted through the gentle details and soft tone.

Her brother is a significant relationship throughout as she describes him as her hero with sweet moments that show him as the ornery older brother while also showing him as her constant protector. Oelerich shares the pain she had losing him which is told through honest reflection. She mentions various types of significant relationships she had throughout her life which range from her family to her pets to friendships to her romantic life. Among the various animals in her life that left an impact are the childhood dog that she told her hopes and dreams to and her cat MoMo that left such a place in her heart that she got a tattoo. Her romantic relationships are delightful and give insight to some amazing moments such as a jaw-dropping affair with Johnny Carson, a tryst with a younger man, and a lovely relationship with her husband Phil.

As she opens up about her life, she also hits upon a subtle commentary about what she's faced which ranges from various moments that involve mention of local gangs in Brooklyn, sexual harassment in the acting industry, and prejudices. Oelerich often reflects on being a young girl that felt like she couldn't do something because she didn't have the same freedom that boys have. She reveals the various dreams she's had in her life as she shares about the various forays she had into acting while also opening up about the sexual harassment she endured from sleazy guys that expected sexual favors in return for the job. She also delves into her true friendships in her life, specifically with Laura who was her friend on her first day of Junior High School and the adventures they had in growing up. Each of these moments she shares ranges from when she was a child to adulthood with the various people that have affected her deeply woven throughout with each moment that touched her life and each one shaping the Memories of a Jewish Girl from Brooklyn.

THE US Review
of Books

REVIEW

BOOK TITLE: **MEMORIES OF A JEWISH GIRL FROM BROOKLYN**
AUTHOR: **HELENE MEISNER OELERICH**

REVIEWED BY: Donna Ford

"Every time I did my homework, I would save my literature or writing or reading for last. That was my dessert."

Oelerich was born to a Jewish immigrant family. Her Russian grandfather arrived as a blacksmith. They fled to America to escape from the Czar's anti-Jewish pogroms. These were violent massacres that targeted religious groups, especially Jews. Working as a blacksmith, her grandfather shoed horses for the NYC police department.

The author's early childhood in Brooklyn is told in chapters 1–4. The author had one older brother she greatly admired. Her father was a paper hanger. Her mother read books to her as a child. When she wasn't reading, Oelerich went to afternoon movies. As a teenager, her activities centered on making her dream to become an actress come true. She studied music and the theatre, including pantomime, taking the bus over to Greenwich Village. During Oelerich's high school years, her mother was a saleslady in Downtown Brooklyn; they both loved City Music Hall and going to the top of the Empire State Building. A close high school friend, Laura, invited her to come along with her family. Laura's mother was an actress. With them at a famous restaurant, the author met Johnny Carson. For a time, they were a couple pursuing more than a casual relationship as he divorced from his first wife. Later, Oelerich was involved in her own failing marriage. Prior to this point, her life dream had changed to teaching children. The author met Phil Oelerich who became her second husband. The couple has been married for twenty-three years.

The author presents her credentials for writing this memoir in the introduction: "I was born, lived, and taught in Brooklyn. New York City is my playground. I am intimately involved in restaurant dining. I live and teach in Whitestone, today. The Throgs Neck Bridge is my backyard." This bridge connects the boroughs of Queens to the south with the Bronx to the north. Five boroughs make up New York City. To a reader who is not native to NYC, the stories in this memoir demonstrate the humanity and welcoming character of neighborhoods within what may seem to some to be a very impersonal city.

The author and her husband live in Queens; they dine at fabulous restaurants and enjoy all that New York has to offer, especially the theatre. For over ten years, she has reviewed restaurants, admittedly covering only restaurants that she likes. Her written reviews appear in magazines and newspapers. For those who already know Oelerich as "The Dining Diva," this memoir serves up another tasty slice of NYC.

Each chapter resembles a short story with a specific theme carried along over several pages. These stories appear to have been written on different occasions. With twenty-plus chapters, there is an understandable overlap of characters and content. A final edit could have polished the entertaining and insightful memories into a cohesive whole for a new audience. Oelerich's own photographs accompany the short stories in this memoir. As explained in Chapter 22, travel and photography are other childhood dreams she has been able to incorporate into an amazing life.

Acknowledgements

1. Dr. Gloria Faretra is my wonderful neighbor. She read my Memories and convinced me to publish my book. She is quite amazing and I love her!

2. I wish to thank Kalito Brown, a student of mine from PS 181, in Brooklyn who recently wrote on Facebook, "Thank you for being my best teacher out of PS 181 … I will never forget Helene Oelerich."

3. I Thank my Son, My Husband, my Friends and Family who are so awesome!

4. I would like to acknowledge Ines, my hair stylist who came to my house and shaved all of my hair off. She also continued to keep my wig clean and pretty. I am a six year survivor of breast cancer as of March 2017!

MY BIO:
HELENE MEISNER OELERICH

I am a daughter, student, teacher, mother, friend, and partner. I am an avid reader, traveler, writer, photographer, and lover. I love animals, tasting great food, loving and being loved, shopping, and exploring the world. I enjoy photographing things and people that mean something to me.

I was born, lived, and taught in Brooklyn. New York City is my playground. I am intimately involved in restaurant dining. I live and teach in Whitestone, today. The Throgs Neck Bridge is my backyard.

My husband is so *very* special. My son is amazing. I share my life with them and my friends.

POEM
A View of the Bridge Evening

Nighttime, spaced out.
Out of the window.
Lights from the bridge sparkle off the water.
Celestial visiters –
Lights move with waves and straighten again constant darkness.
Life in the water, on the water.
Lapping up onto the beach.
Bridge – strong in the water.
Hiding underneath.
A storm – rowboat smashed against the wall.
Water swirling, crushing, angry
Hurricane over, over, on top of
Up the beach, to the walls. Licking the walls
Anger overtaking, whirlwind-chaos, round and round over again and again.
Light – slowly the sky breaks

lifts, opens, morning, mourning.
Quiet – the ocean compromises the sky. Calms, stills,
will come again when it's ready.
The moon, so clear, so ripe
Cool, warm, bright, contented, steady.
Stars – bright, dark, satisfied ocean.
Evening – a sparkling creation—mine!

I've always had an overactive imagination. I used to dream about getting lost in strange and exotic places. I dreamt of flying and biking and running through forests and deserts and cities with unfamiliar names and interesting-looking people and animals. I read every book I could get my hands on. Libraries and bookstores were my special places. I was thrilled with the possibility of traveling and meeting and getting involved in new experiences. Sometimes I had strange and scary dreams. Always wanting someone to come and lead me, to introduce me, to help me conquer my fears.

I'd wake up breathing hard, scared and confused. I'm a child and having the same dreams again and again: Walking along a quiet, sandy beach road, sun shining into my soul. It feels delicious to smell the summer air and listen to the waves as they lap up onto the shore. I keep walking. The waves come up on my right and on my left! The distance is endless. I look behind and see the lone road fading into forever. Someone help me! The water is beginning to reach me … on both sides. How will I escape?

Another dream: The train is roaring past the station. It shoots through time. The noise is deafening. It expands and speeds, rumbles, and roars. At the exact same time, I am moving in slow motion. I am walking by the side of the train. I hear the crawl of a clock, painstakingly slow. Moving like a turtle's exploration of the earth. How to coordinate … how to align … I'm going to explode!

As a teenager, I combined my dreams into one of becoming an actress. I studied at the Bank Street Theatre and entered beauty pageants. I dated directors and actors and enjoyed all the theatrical events NYC is famous for.

I found that writing poetry and short stories was both rewarding and therapeutic. I wrote into the night and felt like I was galloping through my Brooklyn-identified sensory overloaded existence.

My acting career was short-lived; however, teaching children how to enhance their lives on the stage at our school became a satisfying and interesting career for me.

Going to many schools of higher education and learning was also a great stimulus and added to my dreams of fulfilling fantasies and defying fears and keeping up with it all.

And traveling the world over—to China and Scotland, Paris and Aruba and beyond. Finally my dreams come true.

My appetite and curiosity about restaurants in the most wonderful city in the world—NYC— allowed me to review the restaurants and becoming known as "The Dining Diva."

My love of nature gave me the opportunity to become a photographer.

My love of men and incredible sexual fulfillment brought me to date, marry, divorce, and finally find my true love.

This book is my story.

CHAPTER 1

HOW I FELT ABOUT MYSELF AS A CHILD

I don't remember thinking about how I looked when I was very young. I know I felt happy. I had a mom who read books to me and played cards with me and always told me I was wonderful. I loved to read more than anything and always said reading was my hobby. By the time I was ten, I had read all the Pollyanna books and anything else I could get my hands on. Going to the library was a favorite treat. Being surrounded by books was intoxicating. Buying my own book from a bookstore or receiving one as a present was reserved for special occasions. I felt pleasure from the scent of the book's pages and luxuriated in my bed at night curled up with a book in my hands. My mom had to push me out the door in the summertime. Once there, I would read on the stoop or in a chair in the backyard! When I wasn't reading, I would go to the local movie theatre, where the most fascinating movies took me to paradise.

I had an older brother who teased me and flipped me onto the bed and held me upside down, saying, "Little girl for sale." As I grew up, he was more conscious of my looks than I was. He told me to brush my hair a hundred times a day. He let me know when he thought I should wear a bra. Sometimes I felt embarrassed; mostly I felt cared for.

I was five when he was bar mitzvah. My mom curled my hair in rags so I could wear it long around my face. Once, she put a bowl over my head and cut my bangs. It looked awful and took a long time to grow out.

My dad worked a lot and so I watched him when he was home. I watched him shave and fold his clothes and put shoe trees into his shoes and wash his car on Sundays. I watched him read the *Daily News* and eat Virginia ham sandwiches. I wished I could be closer to him.

I watched my mom "put on her face." I tried on her make-up and laughed. My mom walked me to school and picked me up when I was very young. I came home for lunch too, and we often watched soap operas or read comic books while I ate. It was a happy time. When I was eight years old, I started to eat lunch at school. My mom took a job as a saleslady at A&S in Brooklyn. She took me shopping there and to Mays Department Store. We didn't have a lot of money; however, she made sure I had stylish clothes. We always had so much fun shopping and having lunch together.

I was a skinny girl with big brown eyes, curly hair, and clear skin. I hardly ever had a blemish and my teeth were naturally very white. I had nice ears and perfectly shaped eyebrows. I never shaved as I hardly had any hair on my body. I was very lucky. When my body ached with fever or a stomachache, I was treated to hours of comfort and care. It was special to be sick in my home. When I felt pleasure by rubbing my body against the bedpost, my mom said I would hurt myself, but I knew it felt good. When I got my period at age 10, she told me not to let any boys touch me or I could get pregnant. It bothered me that she wasn't more sensitive. From that day on, she trusted me to do the right thing, and so I often felt guilty if I went too far.

CHAPTER 2

SCHOOL BEGINNINGS

"Step on a crack, break your mother's back!" Mom let me walk a little, holding my hand. We were going to elementary school. She carried me across McDonald Avenue in Brooklyn, New York, where there was lots of traffic. I was about three years old. My brother was in fourth grade. The principal had called Mom in again. Irv was always in trouble. We went into the school, the very school where I would go when I was five.

We waited for the principal. She was dressed in a long black dress. I was scared of her! She had one giant shoe and one regular one. My mom whispered not to be afraid. She said the principal had one leg shorter than the other. The principal told my mom that Irv had brought razor blades to school and used them to cut off the ponytail of the girl who sat in front of him. Mom looked really upset. My brother was in the principal's office. Mom told him, "Wait till your father comes home and hears about this!" He looked ashamed. I was thinking, *I don't like this school.* I also giggled because what he did was so strange and sounded so silly and funny! I felt sorry for my brother. He was going to get yelled at, again, but in spite of everything, he's *my* brother and I was not mad at him! Even though he did try to sell me when I was a baby. He even held me upside down, by my feet, and yelled, "Little girl for sale!" But no, I was not mad anymore. I do love having him for my brother.

"Step on a crack, break your mother's back!" I said it over and over again, as I danced around the cracks of the sidewalk. I was then a student at elementary school PS 230. It was lunchtime at school and I was going home for lunch. I felt so grown up. I had memorized the way home. Our apartment house was right around the corner from my school, across from the entrance to the IRT subway. Continue past the big apartment building on Albermarle Road. Turned the corner near Dr. Krammer's office and walked past Mr. Stewart's house straight to 274 East Second Street. Up the steps—"Oh, I got 100 points for playing stoopball yesterday—I hit the top step." "Oh, I wish I could read on the stoop." Mom let me when it's warm out. Push open the iron-gated door. "Ouch, be careful, I remember when I got my fingers crushed in there!" Past the mailboxes, through the door to our apartment at the end of the hall. I made it!

Finally, lunchtime! Mom made a bowl of soup and half a sandwich, usually tuna fish. Everyone loves Mom's tuna fish—Hellmann's mayonnaise and Bumble Bee tuna. Yummy! While I ate, I read comic strips in the *Daily News*. "Dondi" was my favorite. Sometimes we watched a soap opera on TV. *Love of Life, Search for Tomorrow* was our favorite.

One day Mom walked me to school. Outside, the weather was really bad. She helped me put on warm, heavy stockings that had to be held up with a garter belt! They were really uncomfortable. I didn't like to wear them! As we reached the first corner, the water in the street had turned to ice. Mom stepped into the gutter holding my hand and down we went, sliding almost into the middle of the street! "I must be crazy!" she yelled. "It's not worth it! We're going home!"

"Yeah! What a treat!" A whole day without school and I could be cozy in a warm house.

We watched the snow fall through large back windows that faced a huge empty lot filled with trees. Trees that I used to think grew money. I had often heard my parents say, "Do you think money grows on trees?" I thought, maybe? Later, hot chocolate and Mom reading yet another chapter of *Annie of Green Gables*!

"Step on a crack, break your mother's back." School was good. I was the best in reading. However, being home with Mom was even better!

CHAPTER 3

MY PRAYERS

When I was a little girl, I closed my eyes, knelt on the floor beside my bed, and said this prayer:

Now I lay me down to sleep. I pray the Lord my soul to keep. And if I die before I wake, I pray the Lord my soul to take. God Bless Mommy, Daddy, and Irv. Grandma and Grandpa and Penny (our puppy).

Sometimes I would add the name of an aunt or friend or a neighbor who was sick. I didn't like to say "I pray the Lord my soul to take." I was always a little upset that I might die. My mom taught me this prayer, and being a good little girl, I said it whenever it was time for sleep.

I prayed many times for many things as I grew up. My brother was eight years older than me and I prayed that he would stop locking me in my room. Whenever our parents went out on a weekend night, Irv would invite his friends over. They would listen to music and dance and play "Spin the Bottle." Since my bedroom was at the very end of a semicircular-shaped apartment and the bathroom was located at the front, near the front door, I would have to walk the entire apartment to use the potty. Irv had a great idea. He stuck a chair under the door of my closed bedroom so I couldn't get out.

I heard blues and jazz and music from Frank Sinatra. I heard giggling and laughing out loud. Sometimes my prayers would come true. A pretty young teenage gal would want to see me and hug me. "Oh, you are so cute. Come take a walk with me. Do you want a drink? I'll take you to the bathroom. How about a cookie? Look, everyone, Irv's sister is up!"

I prayed for a piano. In the evening, there were several musical shows on TV. I wasn't able to stay up too late; however, I could see the TV from my little bedroom and I loved the sound of the piano.

"Mommy, please let me have a piano. Irv plays the trumpet and I want to play the piano. I'll practice and it'll be so much fun!"

"There is no room for a piano, and besides, it's a lot of money. How about if I get you an accordion? That you can fit anywhere and you will still be playing on keys, like a piano."

I didn't want an accordion. I was a small girl and very skinny. The thought of putting an accordion on my chest was simply awful! I never did get my own musical instrument but I did get to listen to Irv practice his trumpet, day after day. Sometimes it sounded pretty good. Other times it was shear torture.

Mom felt bad about not getting me a piano. She offered to give me dance lessons and I said yes. I took tap, ballet, and acrobatic lessons at a neighborhood dance school. I loved it.

"Guess what? We're going to perform at the Brooklyn Academy of Music at Christmas time. I can't wait!" We were all so excited. "Step, shuffle, ball change … ," I repeated and practiced day after day.

When the time came and the rehearsals were finished, I stood behind the closed curtain on the huge stage of the academy. We all held hands and waited for the music to begin and the curtains to open.

"Smile," whispered the teacher. "Here we go!"

It was breathtaking. We were so good and so cute and so happy to hear the applause from the audience. I still remember seeing my grandmother sitting in the front row, holding a large bouquet of flowers for me. Wow! That was exciting.

I was an avid reader. Mom read to me from the day I was old enough to hold a book. By the time I was four years old, I wanted to read all the books she read to me, like *Annie of Green Gables* and *Pollyanna*. I prayed for gifts of books when it was my birthday. Mom and I would get on a bus and travel to a bookstore in Borough Park, Brooklyn. There, I could choose my very own book.

"I'm going to look around and see what I want. Oh, they smell so good, and look at the covers, so beautiful." The sweet perfume of those first books remains with me to this very day.

I adored stories that took place in China and Africa and in all different regions of the world. I found love stories and mysteries and adventure stories. I read novels that took place in America's South, crying about the prejudice there. I read about the Western states and the Native Americans' struggle and injustices to them. I talked to friends and family about all the issues I learned about. I liked feeling grown-up and discussing world events.

Getting into bed at night with a little light and sometimes a flashlight under the covers, I would read and enjoy and revel in the lives of my fictional characters, as well as real ones in the news.

I also cherished going to the library. It was heaven on earth for me. I could stay there for hours at a time. When I was old enough, I walked to the Kensington Branch on McDonald Avenue in Brooklyn, by myself. I borrowed all the books written by Pearl S. Buck about her travels to China and the Orient. I prayed that someday I could travel to different parts of the world and meet the kind of people I met in my books.

When I was about eleven years old, I had to pass Scarolas Italian Restaurant on Church Avenue and the pool parlor above it. This was around the corner from our apartment on East Second Street. I was on my way to the library when I saw one of the Gallo brothers, Joey, a famous gang member. He was standing outside Scarolas smoking a cigarette. He saw me coming, scooped me up into his arms, and carried me into the restaurant. He insisted on buying me a soda. He surprised me by knowing my whole family history as well as our names and address.

"If anyone bothers you, you let me know! I'll take care of them … okay … you know … Don't forget! And when you graduate, I'm taking you to prom!" All I could think to say was "Okay, thanks!"

Gangs were big in Brooklyn and in other boroughs at that time. Many gang members were often written about in the newspapers. Unfortunately, a few years later, Joey was shot dead and many of his friends and relatives were put in prison.

I prayed that I could eat ices. My mom believed that eating ices could make you sick. "The ice cream man is here! Quick, before he leaves. Please let's get ices this time!" The Good Humor Man was a beloved character in our Brooklyn neighborhood. "You can have ice cream," Mom said, "but no ices … It will give you a sore throat." When I was nine years old, my father's brother Uncle Al, an MD, took out my tonsils. He told my mom to give me ices every day for ten days. My prayers were answered. When we heard the bells ringing the very next day, Mom rushed out to the Good Humor Man and bought me ices. I had a different flavor each day. Heaven!

I prayed for a puppy dog. Both my parents worked and didn't want a pet. "Please I'll love it forever, and I promise to walk the dog … please…" This went on for a few months, until one night a robber broke into our kitchen and stole my dad's wallet. There was a large window in our kitchen that faced an alleyway. Dad had left his wallet on the kitchen table. That's when we got Penny, a collie and fox terrier mix. She was a medium-size dog with lots of fur and the intelligence of a terrier. Her fur was caramel and dark brown. She had sweet ears and dark brown eyes. Her fur was long and soft like a collie and she shed all over the place. She loved to be brushed and would run all around the house after being bathed in the bathtub. I loved her with all my heart and soul. Best of all, according to my parents, was the fact that she barked at the slightest sound outside. Truth be known, she barked and hid under the bed if someone approached. However, the barking scared away anyone who was up to no good.

Sometime around twelve years old, I stopped praying and wished and wanted for a lot of things. I wanted someone to come and take me to far off places around the world. I wanted bigger boobs when I saw how guys would stare at large breasts bulging out of some girls sweaters at school. I wanted to become an actress.

My close friends—Laura, Eileen, Sharon—and I looked forward to Saturday afternoons when we went to the Bank Street Theater School in Manhattan for drama lessons. We were twelve years old and so excited to take the train from Brooklyn into Greenwich Village. Bank Street was famous for training actors. As we entered the building and climbed the steps to the lobby, we instantly found ourselves in a whole new world. Everyone was going to classes, learning their lines, discussing which big star they had just seen, and dreaming of becoming successful in the world of theatre.

We met out teacher, the famous Uta Hagen, and sat in a makeshift audience with scripts in hand. I began with pantomime and had fun standing on the stage and feeling the excitement rush from my toes all the way through my head. I was nervous. What if I forget what to do? I didn't want anyone to laugh at me unless I was being funny. We moved about, learning the various terms applied to the stage. We performed from several one-act scripts and had assignments to memorize our lines for the next session. We all loved being there, and afterward, we would have lunch at famous coffee houses, where we believed we felt the vibes of poets and musicians who had written and in some cases were still writing their works of art. I even took speech lessons to get rid of my Brooklyn accent.

When I was thirteen years old, my brother graduated from college and joined the army. He was sent to Alaska. He was so amazing in his abilities that he was put in charge of a large group of soldiers to train and work with. At some point in his two years away, he won a fishing trip to a nearby area as a reward for his good work. He wrote quite often and told us about his adventures. He also told me that after being in such a freezing environment, he was considering moving to California when he left the army. I was not happy about that and hoped he might change his mind when he got home. While there, he submitted my picture for an army beauty contest and I came in second place. I received an award in the mail and felt very honored.

When Irv returned home, I was thrilled to see him and be with him. He took me out for a day in Manhattan. He held my hand as we walked past Wolman's ice skating rink. We went to see a movie and had lunch at a restaurant in Greenwich Village. He ordered turtle soup and I ate it only because I was with him. I thought he was the greatest brother in the world.

After a few months at home, Irv decided to move to Los Angeles and begin a new life there. We were sad to see him go; however, my parents wanted him to be happy and have the kind of life he wished for. He had several interviews with IBM, and being a business major with a very high GPA, he was excited to take the job offer.

He was my hero. I didn't think I could ever have the luxury to take off someday and live in another place! I accepted that girls just didn't have the same freedom boys had. I was taught this in everything I read and heard about. It was that time in our history when I believed her-story was not yet written.

Irv returned to visit us whenever his company sent him on a business trip. Our apartment wasn't too far from Kennedy Airport and since we couldn't afford to fly to LA, we looked forward to his every visit. Once he came home with a bad virus. He couldn't wait to lie down in our parents' bed and be treated like a little boy again. I thought this was very funny.

When we grew up, getting sick was quite an experience. We got to spend time in Mom and Dad's big bed. That was a very special treat. Except for the discomfort of the sickness, it was a big joy of our childhood—games, special foods, loving care, and lots of attention.

Mom prepared comfort food and Dad took time out to play checkers and dominoes with us. Since he worked twelve hours a day, this was a big deal. He put aside his tiredness and spent extra time with us.

One time Irv was home when I was at a beauty contest. I entered the Miss Brooklyn beauty pageant held at the Brooklyn Paramount Theatre. I went alone. How surprised I was to hear someone applauding and shouting for me. It was my brother home from another business trip, there to surprise me. I came in the top 10 but was told by the manager of the contest that I would have been number one (the winner) had I been taller. At five foot two, I never came in first place. This time, I was so happy to have my brother cheering me on, I felt like a number one winner.

CHAPTER 4

EARLY YEARS

I grew up in the Flatbush section of Brooklyn, New York. This area, known as Kensington, is a neighborhood surrounded by Borough Park, where my grandmother shopped for her kosher supplies; Prospect Park, where I took horseback riding lessons, petrified of falling and exhilarated at being so tall in the breezy, fresh blowing air and where I skated with my brother and father on the park's beautiful, frozen lake. This neighborhood is also known for Greenwood Cemetery, where many famous New Yorkers are buried, and Flatbush Avenue, once upon a time the shopping mecca for this part of Brooklyn. Going to Flatbush Avenue was the most fun as you had to take a trolley car on Church Avenue that dipped under Ocean Parkway and up Coney Island Avenue before arriving at your destination.

Closer to my apartment was the Beverly movie theater, where Mom went every Tuesday evening to get free dishes with the price of a movie ticket and where I won a bicycle for entering a coloring contest. Don't tell anyone that my brother colored the picture for me! Then there was Netell's Bakery, where Mom and I would buy a charlotte russe to push up in the cardboard container (filled with sweet cake, whipped cream, and sprinkles). Sometimes in the excitement to get the sweet into your mouth, we pushed so hard that it fell onto the sidewalk. Ooooops! We'd also buy a whole loaf of rye bread with seeds only to eat half of it on the way home. Then there was Ebinger's Bakery, famous for its Black-Out Cake; Scarola's Pizza Parlor, where a lot of the mafia gangs hung out; Gorelich's Jewish Deli with the best corned beef and pastrami sandwiches; and the Chinese restaurant where it seemed as if every Jewish family ate chicken chow mein and egg-drop soup on Sunday evenings.

When we weren't eating, there was PS 230, the Kensington branch library (a place of wonder and comfort to me throughout my childhood) and our building with its front and back yards.

I lived on the west side of East Second Street consisting of small six family houses. Every two were attached and most had a yard in the back, sometimes planted with vegetables, sometimes used by me as a quiet place to read. The front of the apartment house has stoops to sit on and steps to walk up.

Many afternoons, when school was out, the stoops would reverberate with the sound of Spalding balls hitting the edges of each step in a game of stoop ball. Yeah, top step for 100 points!

On the east side of the block were small, private homes with wraparound porches. No stoop ball was played there. However I do remember a few games of "Doctor" played behind those quiet houses. "I'll show you mine, if you show me yours!" I also remember getting caught by Mom and having a time-out in the corner of the kitchen at dinnertime when the family sat down to eat.

I lived in a four-room apartment on the first floor with my mom, dad, and older brother Irving. Our apartment faced the backyard, seen through large living room and bedroom windows. Since the back area hadn't been developed yet, we could see all the way to McDonald Avenue, a wide street dividing neighborhoods and busy with traffic. In the winter, my brother and I would take our sleds out to the backyard and have a blast. One time I tried to keep up with Irv and his friends. I went straight into a tree. I had a bloody nose but enjoyed my afternoon in the big bed watching the skaters through a large window while drinking hot chocolate and listening to Nat King Cole on the radio. "Hey Mom, I think this is better."

The outer front door of the building was huge and made of iron and glass. Little fingers sometimes got caught in the fast closing door. "Ouch, I'm bleeding!"

To the right of our apartment door were steps that led to the upper apartments. Neighbors on the upper floors of the building had fire escapes that were often used as escapes from the hot sun and sometimes as a summer bedroom. When my brother practiced his trumpet, they were sure to stay inside, no matter how hot it was.

"OY VEY! There he goes again, shut the windows!"

A stairway down from our apartment door led to the outside courtyard, the center of the two houses that were attached to each other. On the rare occasions that my dad brought home a coconut, he would place it on a newspaper in that stairwell and crack it open with an axe to our utter delight. He also surprised us with Chinese apples, another delicacy. I loved sucking on the red pomegranate seeds.

The door to our apartment, as with our neighbor's doors, was only locked when we went to bed. This door was not very sturdy. It rattled and shook with windy weather and brought nightmares to me then and long after I moved away. Upon opening the apartment door, immediately to the right, there was a bathroom. It contained a makeshift shower in a claw-footed tub under a small window that peeked into the alleyway. I remember watching my father shave in the bathroom and finding sexy novels hidden in the laundry hamper.

One afternoon I was sitting on the toilet when the door swung open. A neighbor, Mrs. Perks, had a whole conversation with me as if we were at a bench in the park together. I was mortified. When she said a nonchalant "good-bye," I vowed to lock that door from then on. Later on, when I was a teenager, Mr. Perks, her soft-spoken gentlemanly husband was hauled away to prison for child pornography. You never know!

As you continued down this hallway from the bathroom, the kitchen came into view. The kitchen was my favorite room in the apartment. It was big and open with large windows facing an outdoor courtyard with leaves rustling around an open drain. Both the kitchen and the smaller of the two bedrooms faced the courtyard. At night, these sounds from the alleyway brought goose bumps to me and scary thoughts into my head as I slept in the tiny bedroom that faced the same yard. In that space, cats would howl and create havoc with their incessant love-making night after night.

I remember the story of the men who took all the cats miles away to the other end of Prospect Park, only to have them all return the next night. We wondered how they knew the way home.

Sometimes, early on weekend mornings, when everyone was finally able to sleep late, the cats would give way to beggars who would sing their songs in the alleyway and catch the pennies wrapped in napkins and thrown to them by the mothers in the kitchens of that house.

Mother was up early, as usual, dressed and ready to go. In the kitchen, the ironing board was out. The clothes that had dried were pulled through the window on a long rope hung from the window pane across the alley to the other side, where Mrs. Taggliterri was getting ready for the day. Mrs. T was known for yelling out the window several times a day in her Italian accent, "Joe, Frank, Giovanni, get in the house! Where are you? Get in here now!"

The radio was on, muffling the noise we could barely hear from the dumbwaiter on the wall. Not used anymore, its presence sometimes hid creepy, crawly bugs that moved through the night. Early on I used it to send notes to Jerry, my upstairs neighbor. "Hey, come and meet me in the backyard. We can play ball." How fun to pull the thick brown ropes and send secret messages into the walls of the house.

I always did my homework at the table while Mother ironed our clothes, sprinkling water and smoothing out shirts and pants and overalls. We listened to the hit parade of songs on our small radio. The same radio brought us Archie Andrews and the Shadow Knows at dinnertime on Sunday nights. It sat on a little wooden shelf on the wall next to a hard salami that glistened with grease and was always ready to be sliced when Father wanted a taste of Jewish bliss! The glow from the kitchen was warm and comforting.

Beyond the kitchen, through a wood and glass doorway, was the living room and Mom and Dad's bedroom. The windows of these rooms faced the backyard. There was no door connecting the living room and bedroom and therefore there was no privacy for Mom and Dad, who slept in the big bedroom. Much to my brother's chagrin, he had to share the little bedroom with me after I was born. I remember him yelling, "Mom, she's all wet again!" When I was born and he realized that Mom couldn't take me back, he tried to sell me. When that failed, we became friends in a teacher- student type of relationship. Sometimes antagonizing me by taking me to see *Frankenstein* (I had nightmares for a month), sticking a chair under my bedroom door so I couldn't get out when he had a party and was playing spin the bottle and then there was Circus-Time where he flipped me onto the bed from his shoulders.

We were somewhat poor, but didn't know it. As children we had what we needed—clothes, skates, games to play, furniture, food, and books. We read the funnies, came home for lunch from school, played stoop ball and the record player. Sometimes Mom and Dad would dance together, their feet intertwined like perfect ballroom dancers. Often Penny, our dog, was jealous of this dance. She felt the intimate connection and wanted to be part of it. She stood up and danced between them, her hind legs jumping, creating a doggy sandwich. We brought Penny home from a neighbor's litter. She was a collie and fox terrier puppy. My parents didn't want the responsibility of a dog since they both worked and Irv and I were in school. However, one night someone crawled through the kitchen window and stole my father's wallet that he had left on the kitchen table. We all agreed that the dog barking alone would keep a robber away. I loved Penny so much. When I was a little girl, I used to sneak kittens into our kitchen by hiding them in my doll carriage. Now I had my own pet who I could tell all my dreams and secrets to while lying on the bed listening to Frank Sinatra songs.

In school, I was in the top reading group and loved to write too. I was nervous and somewhat shy about performing in plays and I remember having to memorize a religious poem and recite it in the school auditorium. It was Easter time and I had to mention the name Jesus. I was afraid to do this. I thought I wasn't allowed because I was Jewish.

Most of my friends in school were not Jewish. I went to church with some girls one Sunday and watched them cross themselves and put holy water on their foreheads. "Oh my God, what will happen to me?" I sat in the back of the church and felt scared. I thought my God would be angry with me.

Later on, when I went to JHS, my body changed and I was forever into make-up and appearance and boys. Stomachaches from guilty feelings (knowing my mom trusted me) often kept me home.

"Will she find out I was necking with that handsome Italian boy on a bench at Ocean Parkway? What if she finds out that the ten dollars I lost on the way to the dentist was because I took a ride on a bike with a boy I just met. He might have stolen it. Oh, my stomach hurts!"

I was always concerned about looking great. If my hair didn't look just right, I didn't want to go to school. I wore a jean jacket with my nickname HONEY written on the back. Everyone called me Honey and I loved the attention. My friends in JHS were of all different backgrounds and economic situations, most of them wealthy. Yet in the eighth grade, I was voted best dressed even though I was the poorest of them all.

Until I went to JHS, my world was at home with my family and the friends that I made in my own neighborhood and elementary school. The only exception was when Mom would take me to Manhattan when there was no school. Mom made sure that her job allowed her to be off from work on school vacations. Being a sales lady at Abraham & Strauss, in downtown Brooklyn, allowed her that freedom and so we visited the Statue of Liberty, Radio City Music Hall, the Empire State Building, and restaurants and shopping. We both enjoyed the excitement of the big city and each other's company.

When I was a teenager, I would lie in bed and dream of someone coming to lead me, to be my mentor, to take me to where I could be the best in anything I wanted. When my brother retuned from the army, I was twelve years old. He had been in Alaska for two years and decided to move to Los Angeles and begin a new life there. I was so sad to see him go. He was my hero. I didn't think I could ever have the luxury to do that! I accepted that girls just didn't have the same freedom boys had. I was taught this in everything I read and heard about. It was that time in our history when I believed Her-Story was not yet written.

CHAPTER 5

MY BROTHER IRV

People remark that I never say Irving or Irv or my brother. I always said and always say, "My brother Irv." I didn't realize that. And it's true! I talk to my brother every day, in my head and in my heart. He will always be my brother Irv. Sometimes he answers me; sometimes I just feel his presence. I don't like that he's not here. I'm angry that I can't change things and bring him back. I like to believe that I'm the kind of person who can get things done once I decided to do something. But this is too hard because I can't do anything about it. It's not fair.

When I was twelve years old, my brother took me on a train from Brooklyn to the city for the first time. He shared his love of Manhattan with me and I loved it too. He held my hand. I felt so happy and so grown up. We walked past the Wolman's Memorial skating rink.

He took me to the movies. The name of the movie was Marty. Could it be that, psychologically, the name was right? In reality the person was not! A lot of things are not fair. I thought I'd be married forever and yet I divorced Marty.

It's been said that when I was born, my brother told our mom to take me back. He had been the only one for a long time and he liked it that way. When he realized I was here to stay, he tried to sell me. He carried me around by my feet. "Little girl for sale," he would shout. He discovered a way to have fun with me. He was the ringmaster in the circus. He would flip me from his shoulders onto the bed. When he babysat me, he slid a chair under the door of my bedroom so I wouldn't get out while he was playing spin the bottle at his party. Once when our mom and dad had to go out, he told me how the world was spinning and how I had to hold on or I would fly off the planet. I was three years old. I was scared; our mother came home to see us sleeping in the same bed and had to pry my fingers from his hair. I was holding on for dear life.

I watched him roller skate, play marbles, stickball, and basketball. He let me sleigh ride in our back yard with his friend until I crashed into a tree and got a bloody nose. He built a racing car and played poker on the weekends with his friends in our house. He loved to paint and draw. He colored a picture for me, which I entered into a contest at the local movie theatre. I won a bicycle. He also took me to see scary movies, like *Dracula*, and I had nightmares for weeks.

We were never in the same schools together. I remember having to go to elementary school with my mom because my brother Irv was in trouble again. One time he cut off a girl's braid that dangled in front of his desk. Another time he stuck a girl's ponytail into an inkwell! I remember going to his high school and listening to him play the trumpet in the school band. I was home in the afternoons when he practiced that trumpet and it was very loud and very annoying.

When he went into the army, I missed him and waited for his letters and tapes. In the beginning, he trained at Fort Dix. My parents and I were allowed to visit him after three weeks. How surprised we were to see him in full uniform, in charge of two hundred soldiers. He was one of the few college graduates to be drafted for a two-year stint in the army. Afterward, he was sent to Alaska to serve his time and won a contest for soldier of the month. He was sent to beautiful Alaska to fish and relax. We were so proud of him! He entered my picture in the Miss Alaska beauty contest. I came in second. However, the fact that he wanted me to enter made me feel like a winner!

Sometime later, I entered the Miss Brooklyn beauty pageant held at the Brooklyn Paramount Theatre. I went alone. I came in the top ten. How surprised I was to hear someone applauding and shouting for me. It was my brother home from a business trip, there to surprise me.

The night before I married Marty, my brother Irv & I skipped down East Second Street, singing, "I'm gettin' married in the morning, ding dong the bells are gonna chime!" Twelve years later, he gave me the thousand dollars I needed to obtain a divorce. He danced with me at my son's bar mitzvah. He gave me away when I married Phil.

My brother set off for California the month after he arrived home from Alaska. He only had $400 and a used convertible car. He knew he would make it there and he did. He became the number one sales man for IBM. When he took vacations, he would go mountain climbing and send home pictures. We saw him waking up in the Grand Canyon, using a cactus for a pillow. He wrote beautiful poetry. He was pictured in a book of most desirable bachelors after his divorce.

When he married his beautiful Chinese girlfriend, I located a Justice of the Peace and prepared a ceremony for them in an office near the city hall in New York City. They stayed at the Plaza Hotel and we celebrated at Chin Chin Restaurant. We were together. It was very special.

Our parents smoked. We smoked. Everyone I knew smoked. All the actors we adored in the movies smoked. Last summer, my brother was diagnosed with lung cancer. We thought we could fight it together. In four excruciating months, he was gone. I went with him to chemotherapy. I cooked and cleaned and stayed with him at his home in Hollywood Hills. I drove in a strange car down the hill to pick up my nephew from Beverly Hills High School and to handle my chores. I was frightened. I was alone. I thought I'd get lost or have an accident. After all, I'm just my brother's little sister. How could I take care of him? And he wasn't easy on me or anyone else. He felt so betrayed. He had stopped smoking in the early 1970s. He had a wife, a home, a young son, and me. He didn't want to die. He didn't want to believe it would really happen. The doctors sounded hopeful. We planned to celebrate his birthday in August, two days before mine. He died in July. His funeral was on my eleventh wedding anniversary. I thought maybe I shouldn't live either. I didn't want to be here without him. I didn't know if I could do it. My brother loved my son Brian very much. Brian was home from Iraq, safe and sound. My husband is wonderful. This has helped me too. My brother's son David will be starting college this fall. He was going to visit schools with his dad. My husband and I took him. This has helped me too.

Our family, as well as many coworkers and friends, were at the funeral. Afterward, we all went to one of my brother's favorite restaurants, Jerry's Kosher Deli in Los Angeles. Most everyone had a story to tell. I wanted to hear my brother's story. I wanted him to tell it. So now, I'm telling it and I think he's listening. I miss him so much!

CHAPTER 6

MY RELATIONSHIP
TO MY FATHER

My father was a quiet, reserved, hard-working man. He was ten years older than my mother and came from a family of four brothers and one sister. He came to America from Poland/Russia when he was three years old and settled in Brooklyn, New York. When I first met my grandparents, I was very young. I remember a large apartment in a two-story house. There were many rooms all furnished in a grand, formal manner. There was a baby grand piano and a Victoria with a giant cone gracefully emerging from the side of the player. There were dark, large pieces of furniture and a small, shiny, lacquered box that held white pistachio nuts. It was the first object I went to after politely saying hello. My grandmother would often be sitting at the head of the dining room table, reading the *New York Times*. She had arrived from Europe at the end of the 1800s, taught herself English, and forged ahead into the world of business. She opened Meisner Wallpaper and Paint Company on Atlantic Avenue in Brooklyn and it became the foremost store of its kind. Very successful, she sent her oldest son to medical school and my father was slated to become a dentist. I don't remember my grandfather. I believed he had a white beard and was a very quiet European gentleman.

One of Dad's brothers, my uncle Harry, was born deaf-mute and learned sign language although he never went to a formal school. He was a very gentle man who loved to comb my hair and mouth words to me. My aunt Ethel, the only girl, was very beautiful and catered to by the boys. My other uncles were businessmen. I had a happy relationship with my father's youngest brother Ben. He was so handsome and funny. He would go for walks with me in his Brooklyn neighborhood and he would hold my hand. He called me his little girl and I loved it!

I was told that my dad was quite a roving ladies' man growing up. He was short, cute, and dressed in the latest fashions. He had a Chrysler Roadster and would visit the speakeasies that were prevalent in New York City during prohibition days. I believe he was what was known a stage door Johnny. He said he always dated girls on the end of the chorus line, as they were the shortest.

This was not the man I remember. He had decided not to become a dentist, but rather work with his brothers. When he married my mom, he worked in the family business. The brothers were all single. They worked twenty hours a day, sometimes sleeping in the store. My mom wanted her husband home. She wanted a normal lifestyle. When my brother was born, my dad had a big argument with his family. He left the business and decided to go on his own as a wallpaper hanger and painter. He was known as the gentleman paperhanger by his customers. The problem was that they were few and far between, as it was a time in our history when people didn't have much money for food, never mind decorating their apartments. From that day on, they didn't have much money.

When my dad worked, it was from 6:00 a.m. to 6:00 p.m. He was always tired and often fell asleep at the table after having his coffee at night. He was a quiet man; however, my parents loved music, and once in a while, they would dance in the living room. They danced ballroom style, and when we had our dog, Penny, she would join them and dance on her two legs in the middle of their embrace. Other than the dancing and an occasional hug, there were no displays of affection that I can remember. Our apartment did not allow for intimacy. The rooms all opened upon each other, and in order to go to the children's bedroom or the bathroom, one had to walk through the master bedroom. I can't even imagine how I was conceived!

When I was nine years old, my uncle, who had delivered me when I was born, took my tonsils out. Two important things occurred. Least important, Mom let me eat ices for the first time. The biggest thrill of this time was when my father carried me into the house from his car. I was still groggy from the procedure, and it was the first time I remember being held by him. It stayed with me for a long time.

My idea of the perfect father side was the TV portrayal of Father Knows Best and my best friend Laura's Dad Max. However as my dad got older, his dry sense of humor was developed, and the playfulness that I had been told he displayed as a young man returned. I particularly enjoyed Sunday outings when we would travel to relatives on Long Island and inevitably get lost. I thought getting lost was the most adventurous time! I always sat up front with my dad, as I was the one to get carsick if I sat in the back. He had a picture of my mom glued to the top of the shift and would say he would get his frustrations out by banging the shift into gear. This was his sense of humor.

Every evening we had dinner together as a family. My dad ate things that no one else did. He ate kipper herring fried with onions. He ate Virginia and fresh ham sandwiches. We had salad and rye toast with mayonnaise every night of the week. I didn't know Jewish families didn't eat like this. My dad loved to eat olives. No one else did. I made it my goal to learn how to eat and enjoy them. This was no easy feat as we all had a sweet tooth, except for my dad who could enjoy sucking on a lemon. I wanted to have something that only he and I shared. I learned to love olives and Dad and I would eat them together while my mom and brother would say "Oooooh, how could you eat them!" Till this day, I love all kinds of olives.

Almost everything that I did my young life at home was with my mom. My brother had a bit more of a relationship with my dad as he went to work with him a few times as a teenager. There were no ballgames or activities that my dad went to with us as children. My parents would attend school functions, but other than that, we played with our friends in our own neighborhood. Inside our home, we read, ate together, rested, played, painted, listened to the radio or TV, and we were a family together.

My parents had no real close friends except for my mom's sisters who would visit often, and other relatives that we visited. My mom's parents and her single sisters lived close by and were very friendly, open, warm people. All the Jewish holidays were celebrated with them. Many dinners were eaten at their home on weekends. My grandfather, who used to be a blacksmith for the NYC police department, would babysit us once in a while, on the unusual occasion when my parents went out by themselves. I overheard my mom say that neighbors shouldn't know our business. She kept to herself except for a polite hello to the neighborhood population. I had heard a story about my parents' wedding. It took place on an extremely hot, over a hundred-degree day in the summertime. My dad's friends didn't come because of the weather. He never saw or talked to them again.

Until I went to JHS, my world was with my family and the friends that I made on East Second street, in the Flatbush section of Brooklyn. The only exceptions were when my mom would take me to Manhattan during every one of my vacations from school. Then it was the Statue of Liberty and Radio City Music Hall and the Empire State Building and restaurants and shopping and the excitement of the big city. My father never joined us. He worked all the time.

Tuesday evenings were movie nights at the Beverly movie theater around the corner. Dishes were given as prizes, luring housewives to attend. Tear-jerkers and musicals were the movies shown. My father stayed home. I went with my mom and the neighbors.

My parents were together for over forty-five years, the last few in Florida, where they enjoyed the warm weather, going to the racetrack, seeing shows, dancing, and having the company of their children and grandchildren when we visited them. Growing up I observed worries my parents had about money and arguments about in-laws, but also laughter and caring and sharing.

I made sure, in my second marriage, that I found a man who would give me all the loving and touching and affection that I need. This I attribute to my relationship with my dad.

MY FATHER

"Oh! Can we really go roller skating?" My dad took me, just *me* to the skating rink at Prospect Park. I was excited to have all of his attention.

A look, that's all it took to make me cry. Mom would yell and it didn't matter. Just one look of disappointment from my father and I would cry.

I would watch Daddy shaving in the small bathroom. He would put the white foam on his face and rub the straight edge razor across a long piece of leather. I liked to watch him shave.

Daddy said, "Your mother is so funny. She cleans up the dinner table and she takes the saucer out from under my coffee cup to wash it, even before I finish drinking my coffee!"

Daddy lingers at the dinner table and often nods and falls asleep for a minute or two before going into the living room to relax.

Mom and Dad dance together in the living room to music played from the record player. Their feet perfectly interactive with each other.

Daddy read the poem, "T'was the Night Before Christmas" every Christmas Eve.

When my brother and I got sick, we could go into the big bed and get lots of attention. Daddy played checkers with us when we were resting in bed.

Daddy read the *Daily News* and the *Post* every day at the kitchen table.

My father loved to eat olives. No one else in the family did. I learned how to eat them in order to have a special connection to him. I wanted to be the one who could share in this with my dad. Kind of a special "olive" club!

Daddy would drive his car and take us out on Sunday afternoons. His car was a source of pride. "Always buy a better one than the one you had before. And keep it clean and shiny," he said.

Daddy said he put Mom's picture on the hand-shift so when he was mad at her he could knock her around. We thought that was hysterical as Daddy was very gentle.

Daddy would get his car cleaned at the local carwash. After he brought the car home, he would then really wash the car!

Mother would say, "Your father never gets out of the house before twelve noon!" I believed that on Sundays Daddy needed to rest in the morning.

My favorite thing was to get lost on these trips to relatives and other festive places. I loved getting lost. It was the most adventurous day!

When my dad graduated from boy's high school, fluent in Latin and with very high marks in all subjects, he was supposed to go to dental school. However, he wanted to work in the family business.

Sometimes, on Sundays we would go to visit my paternal grandparents, so different from my Mom's parents who were down-to-earth immigrants from Russia, warm and loving. My dad's parents were strict and formal and ran a large wallpaper and paint business in Brooklyn called Meisner's Wallpaper & Paint. Grandma would sit at the dining room table reading the *New York Times*. She was self-taught and ran the family business. They lived in a two-family house. I remember the large dining room and the wooden table on which was found a shiny, black-lacquered dish that held white pistachio nuts. I went straight to remove the cover of that special treat as soon as I gave the obligatory kiss to Grandma. In an alcove was an old gramophone. It had a hornlike protrusion from which music floated out into the room. There was a picture of a dog and written on the funnel were the words: "His Majesty's Voice RCA Victor."

My father's three unmarried brothers lived with their parents. Another brother named Adolph was a doctor and a beautiful sister named Ethel moved to California after marrying a businessman who became a famous Beverly Hills store owner.

There was animosity in the family stemming from an argument about work. Daddy said he was cut out of the business because he wanted a family life. My uncles worked day and night sometimes even slept in the store. My little girl perspective remembered that my uncle Harry was mute and he loved to comb my hair. My Uncle George was all business. My Uncle Ben was so handsome and would take me for walks in the neighborhood and hold my hand. I don't remember my grandfather. I think he was very old and had a big gray beard. Later on, I thought it was funny that my grandparents were named Mary and Joseph and they were Jewish!

Daddy told us that he used to go to Speak-Easies when he was dating. He said he would wait with his friends outside the entrances of the theatres on Broadway to meet the chorus girls. He said he dated one of the chorus girls on the end of the chorus line because she was the shortest and Dad was only five feet four inches tall. Daddy drove a Chrysler Roadster when he was single. It had a runner seat on the back of the car and a running board on both sides. Daddy told us he was stopped by the police for not being old enough to drive a car. At the time, he was thirty years old.

Daddy often ordered Virginia ham and cheese sandwich for lunch. He liked an ice-cold beer in the hot summer. I didn't know that most Jewish fathers didn't do this.

When I was nine, Uncle Adolph took out my tonsils. When I came home from my uncle's office, my dad carried me into our apartment. This was a very special day. Not only could I now have the ices I had been denied all my life, but my dad held me while carrying me inside! In our house, no one kissed or showed affection of this sort. I never forgot that moment.

"Your brother has book knowledge but you have common sense and are a lot more sensitive!" My father said this when we were alone. This was in reference to my brother declaring that his own problems were more significant than ours because what he was into was a lot more important than our everyday issues. I had said that each person's problems were important to themselves equally.

Daddy didn't have many friends. He married my mom on a horrendously hot August day. There was no air-conditioning at that time. His few close friends didn't show up and he never wanted to see them again.

Daddy was referred to by his clients as "the gentleman paperhanger." He always left his job spotless. In the evening, he would fold his work overalls and put shoe-trees inside his paint-spotted work shoes.

When my dad let me borrow his car to go to Brooklyn College, I scraped his back fender. I thought he would be so angry with me. I got some paint and sat on the street curb that night and tried to paint over the scrape.

Daddy would walk Penny, our dog, whenever he came back from a car trip and everyone was tired.

I remember the awful smell of his cigar when it was sitting in the ashtray, not being smoked … Yuck!

Dad's nose was flat in the middle. He broke it when he was a child playing Johnny-on-the-Pony. His parents never thought of getting it set and so it remained broken.

Mom and Dad loved the racetrack. They would go to see the trotters run at Roosevelt Field on weekend nights. Daddy would always show the winning tickets. He never showed the ones he lost!

When I took the EST training after I separated from my husband, I shared the feeling of being loved when my dad carried me into the house after I had my tonsils out. It was the first time I said that to him out loud!

My dad had a gray goatee and a moustache when he got older. He had emphysema from smoking and died when he was seventy-seven. I took my nephew David, who is named after my dad, to

Ellis Island where he made a rubbing of his grandpa's name from the Wall of Remembrance.

I will always call my father "Daddy"!

CHAPTER 7

FASHION PHILOSOPHY

"Be ready in a minute, just have to doll up."

Every day, from the time I was a little girl, I watched my mom put on her make-up before she would leave the house.

Foundation, rouge, lipstick, a comb through her hair, and we'd be off for the day.

The other moms in our Brooklyn neighborhood would be dressed in what Mom called housedresses. She thought that they were ugly, baggy, and unattractive. My mother would wear a skirt and blouse, stockings, and nice shoes all the time.

Mom began to work when I started school. All my vacations and days off were her days off too. She was in charge of a baby department in A&S Department Store and always looked professional.

I believe that I got my fashion philosophy from my mom.

When I graduated from Montauk JHS, I was named best dressed. Mom and I had a good laugh about that. My friends in JHS were, for the most part, very wealthy. We were on the poorer side. Mom and I went shopping on Saturdays for my clothes. We could afford Mays and bargains at A&S.

Mom said, "The way you walk and carry yourself is so important, and when you see an outfit you like, buy it. You can always return it but it may not be there if you wait." As a teenager, all my friends would congregate at my house. They loved to talk to my mom about things they said their moms didn't understand. We all tried new make-up and hairstyles—some quite outlandish. Their moms said no. My mom said, "Why not! It's just a fad. Try it for a while until the next one comes along."

In high school, aside from my good grades, I was nominated Ms. Pin-Up. We had a good laugh about that too.

"It's all in the way you put it together," she said. Learning to express yourself in your own way and believing in your choices was my mom's fashion philosophy and it's mine too.

CHAPTER 8

JHS FRIENEMY

FRIENEMY ~ An enemy disguised as a friend or a partner who is a competitor, shared dislikes/annoyances/disappointments

I have to say that I didn't have frienemies growing up. I spent most of my time with my family, neighborhood friends, and book friends. If I met someone I didn't like or we had too many differences, then I broke off any relationship that might have grown.

I read all the time. I loved or hated or disagreed with my characters in "print." I watched TV and went to the movies.

The good friends I made in JHS were wonderful. There were also gangs in my school and gals who were jealous of me because the older boys would give me so much attention. One girl in particular, named Cookie, constantly irritated me. I only saw her in the schoolyard, as classes were formed by intelligence. I was in the scholastically bright group. She must have been in the "Let me outta here soon as possible" group. She was tough and loud.

In the schoolyard, she would come right up to my face and say things like, "You're fuckin' around with my boyfriend … and you betta watch yourself!"

Sometimes when I was in a classroom with the teacher teaching and all the students around, one of the tough guys would come into the room, say, "Hey Mr. Ward … keep goin', just saying hello…" and proceed to a seat next to me where he would put his arm around me, and whisper in my ear! It was like being in the show *Grease*. I was embarrassed and shocked and flattered at the same time.

In reality, I hadn't even been out on a date yet! Some neighbors told my mom that they heard I was a really "fast" girl and she should keep an eye on her thirteen-year-old daughter.

My mom thought this was hysterical since she knew I hadn't even kissed a boy yet!

We lived on East Second Street in Kensington area of Brooklyn. The tough boys lived "up the Hill" in the Fort Hamilton section of Brooklyn. They would walk down the hill and stop at my stoop where I was usually sitting, reading a book. They flirted and my neighbors watched. It was so funny.

One day, Cookie was extremely confrontational with her pack of girlfriends surrounding her. I was walking in the schoolyard, ready to eat lunch at a Borough Park sandwich shop with my friends. Cookie pushed me hard so that I fell back, and then shouting into my face she said, "You better watch yourself! I'm going to punch in that face of yours."

I didn't like when people threatened me. I stood up to her.

"Are you threatening me?" I said.

"Yeah … so what?" she answered.

I hauled off and smacked her across the face. I didn't think about what I was doing. I had never done that before to anyone. I saw the enemy and I struck out. At that moment (probably saved by the bell) a whistle blew. The assistant principal, Mr. Brown, witnessed my hitting Cookie and grabbed me by the arm, whisking me away to his office where he called my mom to come up to school.

Needless to say, Cookie never bothered me again.

Not really a frienemy since she wasn't my friend; however, she came to mind in searching for someone that had the word "enemy" to her face.

CHAPTER 9

THINGS I DREAMED OF DOING

At a young age, I wanted to be an actress. I studied at the Bank Street School with the famous stage actress Uta Hagen. I found it exciting and fun, but also nerve-wracking. My nervousness brought about a case of stage fright, which resulted in memory loss, not good for an actor. Meanwhile, my girlfriends and I were so excited to take the train into Manhattan by ourselves and walk all around Greenwich Village. It was so cool and bohemian and grown-up. We studied acting together and afterwards we would have lunch at famous coffee houses, where we believed we felt the vibes of the poets and musicians who had written and were still writing their works of art.

As I got older, I tried for several parts and sometimes found myself in dire circumstances when the producers offered jobs. They expected sexual favor or as we would say, "onto the casting couch." This wasn't the age for crying "sexual harassment." You complied or you didn't get the job. Sometimes you complied and still didn't get the job. These guys were so sleazy. I was attractive and smart, but still a Jewish girl from Brooklyn, which made me tough and resilient. I had my own moral code. Or maybe I didn't want the job enough. All I knew was I wouldn't get involved with any of those guys in any sexual way.

At sixteen, I went to have professional photos taken for a possible movie role. My mom waited outside the Manhattan brownstone as I climbed to the top floor. Once there a middle-aged photographer set me up for photos. I was a little nervous and a lot upset when he pulled my sweater up to get a look at my breasts. I didn't tell Mom that part.

At seventeen, I went for an interview with a director who was filming in New York City. His apartment was in Brooklyn Heights. It was huge, beautifully decorated, and overlooked the East River, allowing for a fabulous view of lower Manhattan. I read for the part of a young woman who was falling in love. The director asked me to sit on his lap. He was to play the young man in the script. I read and he encouraged me to put more emotion into the reading. He said, "You're so young. Do you have any experience in love-making? Can you recall anytime in your life that can put you in the right mood?" And so we kissed. He fondled and put his hands between my legs. I stood up and said, "You have the wrong gal … 'Bye!" I should have smacked him. I was discouraged. *Not again*, I thought. "I'll never be able to do this without being manhandled. Yuck!"

Soon after, I did read for a producer at a magnificent apartment in One Fifth Avenue. His name was John. He was polite and encouraging. The part I read was funny and I was excited. We met a few times and were sort of dating. He took me to the Copacabana where we had dinner with Frank Sinatra's son and his girlfriend. It felt surreal. Back at his apartment, we kissed and fooled around and that was fine with me. The next time we met, I was introduced to his partner, Bill Thompson. He was sexy and gorgeous and I flipped over him. He asked me to have dinner with him. Afterward we went to his apartment. We started kissing and holding each other and soon I was under him on his bed. I wanted him, yet I was uncomfortable because of John. I couldn't believe what happened. Here I was dating one producer and in bed with his friend. We were making love when the phone rang. It was John. I thought I was going to die! I had never been in a circumstance like this before. I heard Bill say, "Yeah, she read for me and she's pretty darn good. Oh, we had a bite to eat and then I put her in a taxi. Sure, we'll talk tomorrow."

Oh shit ... Now what! *I thought*.

He hung up the phone and we just flowed into each other and made love in the mixture of frenzy and passion.

Soon after, he did put me in a taxi for my ride home to Brooklyn. I was so upset with myself I started to talk to the cab driver. "I think I must be crazy," I told him. I just had sex with the guy whose best friend is dating me and I feel so terrible. I don't know what's wrong with me." The cab driver said, "Are you okay?"

"Yeah ... I guess so."

"Well, then go home, get a good night's sleep, and you'll know what to do in the morning." When I got home, I called my best friend Laura and told her what happened. "I actually had sex with him!"

She was terrific. I couldn't believe what she said.

"Oh my God, how fabulous is that! What a great experience. Don't worry about it. I know a lot of girls who would like to have your problem."

She laughed and I felt better.

Another time I was offered a "cheese-cake" pictorial (lots of sexy photos and nudity) but I just couldn't do it! Perhaps had I started there, I would have moved up the ranks. I'll never know. Instead I ran for president of the junior year in my high school, was voted Miss Pin-Up of Erasmus at graduation ceremonies, and was content with that kind of notoriety.

Around the same time, I entered a writing contest and was given a chance to perform in a one-act play for Sanford Meisner, the famous acting teacher. I didn't win the scholarship offered to the best actor, but I realized that it was my writing that gave me the opportunity to try out. Here was something to work on and to dream about. Perhaps now was the time for Her-Story to be written.

CHAPTER 10

GROWING UP WITH LAURA AND HER FAMILY

When I was twelve years old, I entered Montauk Junior High School in Brooklyn. On my very first day in that school, I met Laura. She was my age and lived in my neighborhood; however, I only knew the area surrounding my home. I had never been to her block.

To me it was a world apart. Her family and my family had very different lifestyles. Mine was simple and happy, quiet and ordinary. Hers was a kaleidoscope of colors, emotions, edgy and dramatic.

I lived on East Second Street in a two-bedroom apartment with my family—Mom, Dad, older brother and dog, Penny.

The door to our apartment was often left unlocked during the day. At night, the lock shook in the wind and frightened me. There was a small bathroom to the right of the entrance. I remember watching my dad trim his moustache in the mirror of the medicine cabinet. I also found books that had sexual content hidden in the hamper filled with dirty clothes. How appropriate! The bathroom contained a makeshift shower attached to a claw-footed tub. A small window above the tub peeked into an alleyway.

Down the hallway, past a bookcase filled with novels of Marco Polo and other famous adventurers, the kitchen came into view. It contained a double sink, dining table, wooden cupboards, a radio, and a dumbwaiter. Sometimes bugs popped out of that dark hole. When it was sprayed and clean, I used the dumbwaiter to pass notes through the walls to my friend Jerry, who lived upstairs. Next to the radio, hanging from a nail on the wall, was a kosher salami. Once in a while, my dad and brother would slice off a piece to have for a snack.

The kitchen faced a courtyard from a window where Mom would hang clothes on a line to dry. Every so often, on Sunday mornings, a destitute man would come into the courtyard and sing. We would wrap pennies in a tissue and throw them out at him. All the neighbors could be seen in the various windows that faced the courtyard.

There were also two bedrooms and a living room. All of the floors in the apartment were covered with linoleum and the walls had interesting wallpaper and murals. Because my dad was a wallpaper hanger, whenever he had leftover paper, we would have new and interesting designs. The ceiling was made out of tin squares, dating from an earlier time. Originally, folding doors were between the living room and the master bedroom; however, they had been painted over in an open position so my parents never had any privacy. My brother slept in a pull-out couch in the living room, no privacy either, and I had the one small bedroom with a door. My bedroom, originally shared with my brother, faced the courtyard too. I could hear leaves swirling around the drain in the middle of the yard while cats roamed and meowed most of the night. I often covered my head to keep out the noise.

Laura lived in a private home on East Fifth Street with her mom, dad, brother, and sister, grandmother and dog, Pal. My memory of the house brings to mind large rooms, spacious areas, a winding staircase that led upstairs, and lots of beautiful furniture and objects of art. There were four bedrooms upstairs, a huge double living room downstairs, a giant kitchen, and finished basement. The entrance hall was filled with mirrors and paintings. There was a porch around the front of the house with old, rattan furniture and a key hidden under a large flower pot. Inside, the two living rooms had beautiful furniture—expensive and stylish and comfortable. There was a large book case filled with classics and mysteries as well as soft-covered cowboy adventure books that Laura's father Max read to relax from the stress of being a working lawyer.

There was a piano under a huge painting of flowers in a vase. The piano was always being played by Fredi, Laura's mom. I remember her singing and playing her favorite song, "Digga-Digga Dee, Digga Dee, Digga Dee," as well as lots of Broadway hits. The second living room had some of my favorite things in the house. There were two giant vases filled with jelly beans placed beside huge, comfortable sofas, sitting atop striking oriental rugs. Each day I got to choose which color jelly beans to eat first!

In Laura's bedroom, there were prints of Renoir paintings on the walls. I loved the colors and the fabrics and the furniture in her room. I often slept over and felt as if I were in Europe on an adventure.

The master bedroom was amazing. It had a large king-size bed and a day bed under a window. There was a luxurious throw over the day bed inviting you to lie down. To me, the highlight of the room was the make-up table. An upholstered bench covered in textured fabric sat in front of it. It was thrilling to see all the make-up, silver brushes, combs, and magical potions on that table. In another part of the large bedroom, there was a cocktail table. I remember beautiful martini glasses and a silver shaker. There were lovely tea cups and a Chinese pot on top of the table. On the walls were many photos of Fredi and her theatrical family. These photos were also all over the house in various rooms.

In Laura's home, there was a finished basement, a teenager's fantasy. We had parties. We danced with boys and giggled. We played games with the boys, kissed, found nooks and crannies behind washing machines and dryers for necking and petting, and we experimented with life. We celebrated our birthdays, put on shows, laughed, cried, and enjoyed every moment.

My father was a painter and wallpaper hanger. He worked with my uncle George and uncle Ben to build up the paint and wallpaper business started by my grandparents when they arrived from Russia. The brothers had a successful paint and supply store on Atlantic Avenue in Brooklyn and spent their entire lives wrapped up in their careers. My father wanted to work normal hours and be at home with his family and so an argument ensued and he was cut off from the family business. He never received a penny of the family money. Subsequently, my father would leave for work at seven o'clock each morning and arrive home around six o'clock in the evening. He worked hard and alone. He wore overalls every day and paint-splattered shoes. Every night he folded his clothes as if they were expensive garments and placed his work shoes in shoe-trees. He would wear his nice clothes on the weekends, when we went to visit our grandparents. My dad was usually tired at night and most often quiet in a European, conservative way. He showed us very little affection. My daddy read the paper, ate dinner, and often fell asleep at the table.

Laura's father was a successful lawyer with a business on Forty-Second Street in Manhattan. He was charming and friendly and warm and a Maurice Chevalier look-a-like. He wore Bermuda shorts and a straw hat in the summer, which embarrassed Laura and thrilled me. He wore suits with outlandish ties all the time. He was very much in love with his wife and showered her with flowers and affection. I thought he was an amazing man. I thought he was as wonderful as the father from the television show *Father Knows Best*. I tried hard not to compare him to my dad.

Laura's mother was an actress—tall, silver haired, with drop-dead gorgeous clothes and fabulous make-up. Every time I saw her on the screen, I would yell out, "Fredi!" She was an extra in many, many movies, often with famous stars. She was photographed in several magazines modeling one thing or another. She smoked a cigarette with a long cigarette holder. She always waited for someone to light it. She was sometimes aloof, forever egocentric, and the most interesting person I had ever met.

Her mother-in-law, whose house they lived in, was not particularly fond of her. Grandma was an excellent cook and prepared the meals for the household. The kitchen had a table with a cathedral-style wooden bench on one side and odd wooden chairs on the other. Here we would eat home-baked challah, a Jewish bread and taste scrumptious dishes and many exotic foods that I had never eaten before. Grandma was a traditional cook most of the time but would experiment with a variety of spices and sauces, which enhanced the flavor of her dishes. She also spent many hours in her own room sewing and reading. She liked me and I called her Grandma.

My mom was affectionate to her children. She taught us how to read, by reading to us and taking us to the library. She loved to read! When we were three years old, she taught us to play cards; poker and gin rummy. She always had so many stories to tell us. She came from a warm and loving family of two sisters and three brothers. Her mother liked to cook Jewish meals. We enjoyed the holidays at their apartment.

My grandfather was a blacksmith from Russia. After fleeing from Czar's pogroms and other anti-Jewish propaganda, he arrived in America and continued to shoe horses in New York for the NYC Police Department. He was funny and liked to play chess and checkers with us. He would wiggle his ears when we sat on his lap and touched his nose.

As soon as I was old enough, my mom and I would go shopping. I loved shopping with my mom! We always ate lunch first, either Chinese food in a large restaurant overlooking Fulton Street in downtown Brooklyn, or in a Nedick's corner shop where we would eat hot dogs with our orange drinks. After we ate, we would buy something for me. In the future, we would laugh about the award I received for best dressed in JHS. I was the poorest of my friends and bought my clothes at a discount store called Mays. Yet I won! We had style and it showed.

When I began the third grade, she went to work as a salesperson in Lampstons, a Woolworth type store, around the corner from her mom and dad's apartment house, in the Flatbush section of Brooklyn. Later on, she became the head salesperson in the baby department at the Abraham & Strauss Department Store in downtown Brooklyn. Most of my friends had stay-at-home moms, but my mom got up early, dressed nicely, put the house together, and was off to work. She always said she had to doll up when she put on her make-up.

When there was a school vacation, Mom took off from work. She took me to the Empire State Building, the Statue of Liberty, and movies at Radio City Music Hall. We had the best times roaming the city and loving it together!

It was nice to be home too. Mom would iron at the table in the kitchen while we listened to the Hit Parade on the radio and I did my homework. The kitchen was a fun place to be. We would all eat together every night.

Laura and her family embraced me and brought me into their lives. They took me with them to the theatre. Laura's aunt Bunny worked for very important Broadway producers. We often sat on the steps of the stage and saw many Broadway shows free. They had me join them in their home for Saturday evening parties, when the casts from a variety of current shows would all come to visit. They would sing and dance and smoke and talk of exciting things. Gay and straight, black and white, we would all have fun together into the wee hours of the night. They thought I was smart and pretty and sexy and I loved being in their midst!

Laura's aunt Spivy was famous. At one time she had been the owner of a speak-easy in New York City. Later she traveled to Europe where she opened her own Parisian Night Club. When she was in town, she would visit her sister Fredi. Laura and I would sit in a semicircle at her feet as she regaled us with stories of princes and royalty who would come to hear her sing in Paris. We were thrilled to watch her performances in Manchurian Candidate, Hitchcock present, "The Specialty of the House" (on television) and Requiem for a Heavyweight.

In the summer we would all go to Laura's summer home in New Jersey, sixty acres of sprawling countryside, a man-made lake, a blueberry hill, a well to get water from, and two small guest houses spread around their magnificent country home. I shared a bedroom with Laura in the main house. Laura's family took for granted the house they knew and loved. I was in paradise. I would sit up at two o'clock in the morning when everyone was sleeping and stare out the window. I would watch the deer and the birds and listen to the quiet and feel the richness of the house and the lives of the people sleeping in the house who embraced me.

There were parties with scores of actors and horse-back riding and Grandma's meals and nights under the weeping willow trees around the lake, and theatre people dancing and singing every summer until I was eighteen.

Then, Laura and my friends went away to Europe before starting college at NYU. They had the money and could go. I needed to make money. I stayed home that summer and worked for Melody Bra and Girdle Company in the Garment Center of Manhattan. I was fine with this arrangement as my world was full of books, dances at Flatbush Jewish Center, dating, flirting, and having fun. In high school, I elected to run for president of the junior year, and when I graduated, I was voted Ms. Pin-Up of Erasmus. My parents and I were also going on a road trip to visit my brother in Santa Monica, California. Driving across country and meeting him in Las Vegas was a wonderful trip to contemplate. And I had the 87 percent average I needed to start at Brooklyn College in the fall.

CHAPTER 11

SUCCASUNNA, NEW JERSEY

Succasunna, a strange name for a little bit of paradise. Laura's family owned sixty acres of farmland in this out-of-the-way area in New Jersey. On any given Friday evening, in the summer, Laura and I would meet her dad in Manhattan, drive over the George Washington Bridge West along I-80 toward Morristown, and forty-five miles later arrive at their summer home in Succasunna, New Jersey.

Their large house came into view as we drove up the hill, past two smaller houses where other relatives lived. I saw the lush green grass, big willow trees, gentle hills, the lake, ducks, birds, and Pal—their big, happy dog who was a mixed-breed and looked like a black-and-white beagle. From the streets of Brooklyn to the serene, pastoral countryside in two hours, how miraculous!

I shared a room with Laura. It was medium-sized with a bed that we slept in together. The room contained an antiqued desk with high shelves and a drawer that opened to become a writing place. It was dark brown mahogany with a cherry shine, and I loved sitting at it and holding the feathered pens and writing on the tinted pads. My favorite part of the room was the large window that faced out to the side of the house. At night when everyone in the house was fast asleep, I would sit up and look out the window. The moon was so bright I could see rabbits running around and bats flying from one tree to another. It was quiet and smelled of wild flowers and secret mysteries. It calmed me and excited me at the same time.

In the morning, we would all meet for breakfast in the kitchen. All of our dinners were served here as well. The kitchen was huge and took up the entire lowest portion of the house. Laura's grandma ruled the kitchen. She was a phenomenal cook and glamorous in the country as she was in New York City; her Dad Max, personable and charming as always; Hester, her sister, always writing in her journal; and assorted guests would all sit at the giant wooden table in the kitchen. Usually Bunny, Fredi's sister, would be there with her darling, Mel, and often a variety of show business people who happen to be on hiatus from their Broadway shows.

One of the favorite meals Grandma would prepare was a delicious pot roast. The night before Grandma would rub lemon and kosher salt on the meat. When she was ready to cook it, she would rinse off the salt. She would then add a layer of onions into the pot and cover the meat with mustard, ketchup, garlic, and gravy master or soy sauce. It would cook in a Dutch oven for one hour (one side only) at 325 degrees. It made its own gravy and was finger-licking yummy!

During the lazy summer days, we would swim in the man-made lake and sit under the willow trees reading a favorite book or just talking away the day. When the cast of a show would be invited for the day, there would be singing, dancing, and fooling around. Once the entire cast of *Silk Stockings* arrived and champagne and cocktails flowed, music played, and everyone enjoyed the large space providing an impromptu theatre experience.

Outside near the kitchen, there was a well. As we roamed about collecting blueberries for the evening pies, we would stop and fill the tin dipper with the cold well water. It was the best, most refreshing drink I have ever tasted! Sometimes people would come on the land from the nearby dude-ranch and ask if they could ride their horses through the wooded section of the rest of the property. They were always welcome and I loved seeing the tall, magnificent horses they rode on.

Once, Laura's aunt Judy, who lived in one of the smaller guest houses, was in the lake with her four children. She heard a helicopter and saw it coming closer and closer to the ground. She jumped out of the lake and ran for cover. There was no problem; however, we always teased her about how she attempted to save her own life and forgot about her children.

Unfortunately sometimes things are scary in paradise. The road outside their home could be dangerous as evidenced by crushed turtles and not-swift-enough squirrels. They sometimes got caught under the wheels of a speeding car. Tragically, their dog Pal ran out into the road one time too often and was hit by a car and died. This was very sad and upsetting!

Also there was someone scary—Hank. Hank was the caretaker of the farm. He lived there all year long in a small shack on the property. He was something of a hermit. It was said that he did venture into New York once for a fair and wound up trying to get off an escalator that he mistakenly managed to get on. I believe this was an extremely traumatic experience for him. I was told that when the cats, who lived on the farm had kittens, he drowned them rather than have to care for them. Needless to say, I didn't get very close to Hank whenever I saw him walking around!

In the evenings, we would sit on the porch that connected with the living room. I was quite enchanted with the stories told, drinks served, show tunes wafting through the air. Fredi would play the piano and we would all sing. Life felt quite magical!

Always at the moment I had to return home, I felt sad about leaving. However, I loved my family and Brooklyn and Manhattan and knew I would soon return to Succasunna, New Jersey, and my fascinating vacation would resume again.

CHAPTER 12

A TOUCH OF ERASMUS HALL HIGH SCHOOL

HELENE MEISNER
Class Pin-Up

I heard my skirt rip as I slid out the huge window of my classroom in Erasmus Hall High School. "Oh God! My mom's going to kill me."

"I got you, honey."

Richie grabbed my waist and helped me down. Tall and muscular, hair flying in the wind, Richie was sexy and adorable. I liked the feel of his hands on my body. We were known as Richie and Honey for so long. We both dated each other in JHS and then dated many others. Somehow we always gravitated toward each other as friends and "making out" buddies. I had been in my earth science classroom when I heard his tap on the window. Mr. Linus, my teacher, was looking something up in a journal. He had been lecturing in a monotone, alcoholic voice for a half hour. Everyone knew he drank while teaching. I knew it was time to escape.

"Let's go before he remembers that he had me in his class," I said.

Richie and a few others were ready to play hooky and go to the botanic gardens in Prospect Park. It was springtime and the

Oriental gardens were showcasing cherry blossoms. The sun was shining and the sky pristine. Time to go!

Erasmus Hall High School was firmly cemented into the crowded sidewalk of Flatbush Avenue in the borough of Brooklyn. It looked like a giant castle with iron gates and huge pointy spire rooftops. Everyone seemed to get lost at one time or another as we ran for classes along halls filled with curves and stairways leading to several different areas and corners. The courtyard was immense and the statue of Erasmus loomed over it all.

Everyone in school called me Honey. Since JHS my jean jacket had HONEY written across the back. I ran for president in my junior year at Erasmus and had photos of Honey all over the walls of the school. Most of the photos disappeared before I could take them down. I got several phone calls from guys I didn't know who said my picture was pasted on their bedroom wall. I didn't win but I was voted Miss Pin-Up and would be in the graduating year book with the other celebrities.

I was seventeen, in my senior year, and not afraid to cut out and leave the school. Climbing out the window was not my usual method, but kind of scary and exciting at the same time. I would be graduating in another month and we all knew it had been the junior year marks (SATs) that were most important, so we became more casual about school in these last few months. I had an 89 average with a major in English. However, Brooklyn College required a 92 for girls, and I would have to go to school in the evening and get higher marks in order to go to daytime school. I would be working during the day—again. I had been working after school and during the summertime since I was fourteen.

After graduation, my best friend Laura and her family, together with me and my mom and dad, celebrated at Lundy's Restaurant in Sheepshead Bay, Brooklyn. The delicious chowder and warm biscuits together with the best lobster ever was a happy cushion for our new status as high school graduates on our way to college!

Laura and the other gals I was friendly with were all going to NYU in the fall and Europe for the summer. I was going to

Brooklyn College and I got a job in Manhattan's garment center at Melody Bra & Girdle Company.

"I wish you could go with us. I'll write and tell you all about it and take lots of pictures! I'm going to miss you," said Laura.

"Hey, I'll be happy not being in school. I might even meet someone really cool to go out with. See you in August."

I never even thought about going anywhere outside of NYC. I dreamed of going to NYU with my friends, but knew that was impossible because the tuition was out of my league. I knew I would travel someday, but we couldn't afford it now. My parents worked hard and were always concerned about my welfare. We went places like visiting relatives on Long Island and to Jones Beach. There were also Chinese food on Sundays and some special dinners at Lundy's.

Mom was a sales lady at Abraham & Strauss and worked out a deal where she was off from work on my school holidays so we could play in the city together. We both loved going to Manhattan. We enjoyed movies at Radio City Music Hall, boat rides to the Statue of Liberty, and soaring high up to the top of the Empire State Building.

My dad couldn't join us. He worked ten hours a day as a wallpaper hanger and painter. He was quiet and tired but also caring and present on weekends when we would pile into his car and go somewhere.

My brother was eight years older than me and had moved to Los Angeles when he returned from the army. I was twelve years old. After a stint in the army, where he was sent to Alaska for two years, he said he needed warm weather and a new job experience. I missed him. I saw him when he visited on business from his LA job at IBM or when he was in New York on vacation. In our apartment, we were happy to listen to the radio, watch TV, and read comics from the newspaper. We ate dinner together and all of us read many books—all the time.

In my life, I had a lot of attention from my brother, who would hold my hand and go with me to the city when I was twelve years old. I also always was close with my teachers and friends. I was pretty and popular. I was always thin and my friends were annoyed that I never had to shave my legs. I could eat whatever I wanted. One summer, my mom sent me to camp to gain weight. My friends, sometimes jealous, accepted me anyway.

Yes, there were times when I was little and my brother wanted to sell me. And there were creepy men who would stand with their penis hanging out on subway stations and try to touch me on the train—yuck. There was heartbreak with a young love that didn't work out and times when I heard my parents arguing about money. However, for the most part, I was still pretty content. I had my dog Penny, who I loved every minute of every day. I would tell her my secrets and fall asleep on her warm fur. When I needed solace, I would write poetry and read novels. Every time I did my homework, I would save my literature or writing or reading for last. That was my dessert.

CHAPTER 13

JOHNNY CARSON

After a week of working at Melody, I got a call from Hester, Laura's sister. "Helene … Aunt Bunny and I are going to Sardi's for dinner tomorrow night and we want you to come. Maybe you can come from work." Hester was a writer and already out of college. She was funny and very dramatic. She later became the main comic writer for Joan Rivers and wrote several novels. Bunny was terrific and liked to talk with me. We always spent time together at Laura's country home in Succasunna, New Jersey. Several casts of Broadway shows would come to the summer house and perform all around the lake while drinking and having fun. I had been enjoying summer weekends there over the last six years.

I was so happy to go with them to Sardi's restaurant. "Of course, I'll meet you there … looking forward to it. Thank you so much."

The three of us were sitting in the center of a large room known more for its drawings of famous Hollywood and Broadway stars than for its food. After ordering dinner, the waiter came to me and handed me a note. The note was from Johnny Carson. It said,

"I think you are quite beautiful and would love to meet you this evening." He asked if I would please come by his table. When I turned to where the waiter was pointing, Johnny raised his glass of wine in greeting.

Hester sounded surprised. "Why isn't he interested in me? You're just a seventeen-year-old kid!" Soon, a bottle of crystal champagne arrived at our table. "Oh Hester, he's just flirting. It doesn't mean anything." Secretly I was thrilled. Johnny Carson was quite a recognizable star and Sardi's was mobbed. How did he pick me out?

I decided to walk slowly past his table. He was sitting with Ed McMahon and a few other guys. He introduced me to everyone and asked my name. I sputtered out, "Helene—and thank you for the champagne."

Johnny Carson said, "How about getting together after dinner? I know a great place nearby where we can get an after-dinner drink or coffee." I told him I would let him know. I didn't tell him I had to call my mom. I told my mom about the exciting events of the evening. She said, "Now that sounds interesting. I thought going to Sardi's would be the big story. Be careful and have fun. Just don't come home too late." Mom trusted me, always had and often said she knew I'd do the right thing. Because of that trust I usually did.

After dinner, Bunny wasn't sure if she should let me out of her sight and volunteered to come along.

"Bunny, I'll be fine. I told my mom where I was going and that I wouldn't be home too late."

"Promise me you'll call me if you get into trouble," she said. I smiled at her intense concern.

"Thanks for dinner. I'll speak to you both tomorrow and let you know how it went."

"He's much older than you. Better be careful," said Hester. They reluctantly left and waved good-bye.

Johnny and I left together and walked to a Polynesian restaurant on Broadway called the Lanai. We entered a very tropical room with flowers and trees all around. "Hey, Johnny, over here!" came a voice from the side of the room. I was introduced to Earl Wilson and his wife. Earl Wilson was a famous columnist with the *New York Post*, known for his (p.6) info on whatever was happening in a celebrity's life and then some. Scandal was accepted!

They discussed *The Tonight Show* and I was asked to tell about myself. I wasn't going to say, "I'm a seventeen-year-old Brooklyn, Jewish girl who just came for dinner after a week at a very unglamorous job."

I just said my name, Helene Meisner, and that I met Johnny at Sardi's that very evening. I listened to their conversation and was happy to be included. We had a few drinks and said good-bye.

As we left Johnny said, "Let's go to my apartment. I live on Sutton Place not far from here."

He was quite intoxicated at that point and I had no intention of going anyplace but home. He insisted on putting me in a taxi and taking the ride to Brooklyn with me. I believe he thought forty minutes of fumbling and fondling was better than none at all. It would have been fun for me too; however, I could see the cab driver looking in his rear-view mirror every chance he could and I was happy when we arrived at East Second Street. He walked me up the outside steps to my building's door, and in his tipsy state, he proceeded to fall down all the steps to the sidewalk. I looked around to see if any of my nosy neighbors were watching. No one was around. He was okay and we kissed good night.

He said, "I want to see you again, soon. Let me have your phone number." I gave it to him and he was back in the cab. No one had noticed.

The next day, I was excited to go out on my lunch hour and see if Earl Wilson's column mentioned Johnny Carson. Sure enough there it was. It was written: "Johnny Carson was seen last night at the Lanai restaurant with a lovely young lady. We know he took Ms. M home to Brooklyn."

I was so excited. I, me, myself, Helene was mentioned in Earl Wilson's column (even if no one else would know who Ms. M was). Oh my God!

A few days later, a call came to Melody Bra & Girdle. I was trying to hurry through a discussion with my lecherous boss, when my coworkers whispered, "Come quick, it's Johnny Carson!" He called to invite me to the studio where his show was being televised. When I arrived there after work, I was met by his assistant. As I entered the studio, I noticed one of the attendants seating people for the show. He was calling me, "Honey, over here!" I excused myself for a moment and walked over. The young man had graduated from Erasmus with me a few weeks before. "Hey, today is your lucky day. I'm an intern here and I can get you a good seat!" I said calmly, "Oh no problem. I'm a guest of Johnny Carson. We're dating." And I left him staring with his mouth wide open as I was taken to the control room of the theatre. There Johnny spoke to me from the stage and said he would look for me in the audience. I was given a seat where he could talk to me while he was performing. His show was full of funny monologues and interesting guests. I loved being a part of it all.

Afterward we went backstage to his studio. It was decorated like a private apartment. I figured the furniture must be from past shows that were seen by everyone watching television. There was a sofa, cocktail table, lamps, and right in the center of the room toward the back wall was a complete drum set, cymbals, and all. He told me to get comfortable and he left. Ed McMahon came in and introduced himself to me all over again. We chatted about the show and then he left. Johnny came back with a scotch and soda for both of us and locked the entrance and exit to the studio. He obviously got comfortable too, as he was only wearing blue and white boxer shorts and proceeded to sit behind the drums. For a guy of thirty-five he was quite trim and fit. He was funny, charming, and cute at the same time. He began to serenade me—cymbals and all. Actually, he was very good at playing the drums. Meanwhile I felt that I was living through some kind of theatrical scenario.

He lowered the light and joined me on the sofa. We began to kiss and he started to undress me. I was very thin and my first thought was, "Oh, he'll be disappointed when my bra comes off. I'll have smaller breasts than when he saw me with my sweater on." I was wrong. He was hot and heavy. He said, "Don't worry about protection. After my three sons were born, I had an operation to make sure I could never have any more kids."

In my state of sexual frenzy that was fine with me. We made love and I felt as if I were in a novel or at least a Broadway play. We cuddled, then dressed, and said so long. We planned to meet again very soon. Johnny had a boat docked in the NY harbor and wanted me to go sailing with him.

Little did I know that he was still married, and although separated, his wife and her lawyers were watching his every movement. He had cheated on her before and a lot of money was involved in these divorce proceedings.

The next evening the phone rang in my little bedroom on East Second Street. I was reading a novel and listening to a Frank Sinatra album. It was Johnny. He asked if I was happy about last night. He sounded strange, with a throaty voice that was hoarse and whispery at the same time.

"You sound sick," I said.

"Oh yes, I seem to have picked up a sore throat. I hope I didn't give it to you."

"Oh, no. I'm fine."

He asked specific questions about intimate details. I thought it was a bit strange, also perhaps he just wanted to relive the sensations of the night. I was flattered that he cared enough to call. He told me he was going on a vacation for few days and would call when he got back.

The next day I received another phone call from Johnny. This time he said, in a clear, angry, strong voice, "Why did you tell my ex-wife about our relationship!"

We figured out that the previous night's call was from his wife's lawyer, pretending to be Johnny. I thought I would vomit. My stomach clenched and fear made me sweat. What the hell was happening in my world? I explained that there was no way I could ever have met his wife. "Johnny, my life doesn't include anyone you know or are involved with."

"I understand. I'm sorry. I just couldn't figure out how they knew. I must have left your phone number in a place where they could find it. I'm going to be away for a while at The Greenbrier in West Virginia. When I return, I want to take you out on my boat." We said good-bye and he apologized once again.

I was frightened. I needed to talk to Laura. I didn't have anyone to share with. I couldn't tell my family or anyone else without letting them know that I was having sex with a man twenty years older than me. I couldn't say that secret messages were being sent and detectives may be following me. Perhaps I would be involved in the divorce proceedings? I was not totally naïve, but I was still a kid from Brooklyn who never expected to be involved in a famous star's divorce proceedings!

I didn't go boating. I told myself he was much too old for me, too sophisticated, and he drank too much. I did meet him at Sardi's a few more times. One time just the two of us were having lunch and the handsomest man I had ever seen came over to say hello. I was introduced to him and he gave me a hug. I thought I would melt. He was Sidney Poitier and drop dead sexy! Another time I sat with Ed McMahon and Johnny and others from the show. The jokes were continuous as was the drinking and the flirting. Ed was the worst of all. He was married; however, not one woman could walk by that he didn't sexually accost with his words or actions. Johnny assured me that his divorce was pending and I had nothing to worry about. He flattered me and tried to convince me to come to his apartment. This did not happen.

Later, at the end of the summer, when my friends arrived home from Europe, I clued Laura into all my summer drama. I brought her to Sardi's and introduced her to Johnny. At the end of the summer, my brother came to visit. I immediately took him to Sardi's, and of course, he met Johnny too.

I never went out with him again. He called once more and I told him I was seeing someone else. I've often thought how my life would have changed had I married him or even divorced him.

I've been told that his ex-wives looked like me and were my type. Soon after our relationship ended, he met someone who did resemble me. They were married for nine years before they divorced. She received nearly half a million dollars in cash and art and $100,000 a year in alimony for life. Oh, the money and the fame, however, now just a memory, fifteen minutes of fame, of a teenage interlude full of adventure and experience.

CHAPTER 14

EMBARRASSING SITUATIONS

Separated from my cheating husband, exhausted after throwing him out of the house, weeks of immersing myself in EST (Ehrhart Seminar Training), and borrowing money from my brother to get a divorce, I finally felt my sexual urges returning. I was letting go of the anger from finding the rent money used for gambling debts and learning about all the women he was having sex with from a friend at the school I was teaching in. Now I felt a sense of entitlement.

Being a mom of a six-year-old doesn't allow for much free time; however, my neighbor David lived one floor down from my apartment and was so absolutely adorable. His sister Jody babysat for me and her college-bound brother often came upstairs to say hello and chat. One thing led to another and we enjoyed sexual engagement on those rare occasions when I was alone. "I can't believe we are together like this," David said over and over again. "I dreamed about this but never thought it would come true!"

Before separating from my husband, I remember lying in bed with him and hoping he wouldn't even touch me. Even though I didn't know the extent of his infidelities, I knew something was terribly wrong. He couldn't be trusted. The bookies were calling; he was late all the time and constantly making excuses.

At a post-EST seminar called "Be Here Now," I met Phil. He had also taken the EST training and I felt a wonderful freedom, both sexually and mentally, when I was with him. His first words to me were "I'd love to get to know you ... You have a great ass!" Ha! He was nine years younger than me, extremely caring and loving. We dated. We had sex so often that I met my girlfriend Sandy at the Museum of Modern Art and had to stand while we had lunch. I was too sore to sit! (She still brings that situation up today.)

I was not at all ready for any committed relationship and I let him know that. I wanted our relationship to be totally upfront. He often said, "I thought I wanted to have a wife someday, but I forgot to add … not someone else's." On our third date Phil said, "I'm not leaving you unless you tell me to go. I want to marry you someday so … when you're ready … you let me know!"

Since I was a teacher studying for my master's degree at Queens College, I came into contact with many other teachers and professors. At the same time I was struggling with a lack of money, a lack of time for studying and teaching and giving my all to my adorable and bright son. While Phil was away on vacation, I caught the attention of one of my college professors. He asked me to go to dinner with him. We dined, we laughed, and we came back to my apartment. My son was on one of his rare weekends with his father. The professor and I made love over and over again. He was handsome, intelligent, and great in bed in a totally different way than Phil. When he went to the bathroom I called my friend and said, "Yikes! I'm in bed with my professor. I must be crazy!" Sandy said, "You are crazy. You're calling me at three in the morning!"

A week later Phil returned from his vacation. I had been invited to a party at my babysitter's mom's new apartment. I looked forward to sharing an evening together with her and her friends. Phil said he'd love to go. On our way there, I thought of my recent relationship with Gloria's son. I didn't suppose he would be there.

Upon entering the new apartment, every sense in my head and heart began to buzz. "Uh-oh." I smiled and said hello, kissing everyone and introducing Phil to the other guests. I acted cool and innocent.

Shit, *I thought*. I can't stay here.

"Hi, good to see you. How's school?" David asked. "This is my friend Laura."

"Hi, Helene," said the professor. Just my luck! How in the world did Gloria know him? *I thought.*

"I was going to call you to set up a time to discuss your thesis and help you choose a topic." I needed a drink—right away!

After a short while of petty talk and several glasses of wine, I found my way to be alone with Gloria.

"Gloria, I'm so sorry that we have to leave early but I just can't stay at a party where I've recently had sex with three of the men here. I'll speak with you tomorrow. Thanks so much. Goodnight."

"Good night, everyone. We had a previous commitment. Hope to see you all soon!"

As soon as we left, I took a large breath of fresh air … for the first time that evening. However, I was not looking forward to answering the puzzling looks I was getting from Phil!

CHAPTER 15

GONE CRAZY

Walking into the IRS office, I straightened my shoulders, smoothed down my white clingy sweater, and smiled. I had every intention of getting the money that was owed to me. The middle-aged man, wearing a slightly wrinkled blue dress shirt and gray suit pants, smiled back and asked how he could assist me.

God knows I needed help! The day before I had a shock as I left my teaching job at 3:00 p.m. to get into my car and drive home from Brooklyn, New York, to Whitestone, Queens. This, being my every day schlep, was an accepted activity. To my surprise, my car was not there. After running back into school and calling the police, I discovered my car had been repossessed and would be sold at auction. I only had one payment left and the car would have been 100 percent mine! My soon to be ex-husband had used my car as collateral to take out a loan that he didn't pay back. Both of our names had been on the car. Crazy!

"Thank you ... I must ask you why I did not receive my paycheck when I returned to work after the summer vacation."

In the NYC public school system of the 1980s, teachers received pay every month from September to June and then in September for the summer months. I had been told that my paycheck was confiscated by the IRS. Since I did not get any child support and had been to family court three times to fight for it. I needed my paycheck. The past weekend had me in the parking lot of my apartment complex with my seven-year-old son, trying to figure out what was more important—stamps or toilet paper?

After checking my paperwork, the IRS worker said, "You and your husband have filed a joint tax return and I hate to say this but he owes back taxes."

"Why don't you take the money from him?" I asked. "He's a physical therapist and has his own office."

"Aha, and that's exactly why! He is self-employed and you are easier to get the money from!"

Okay, I thought. *Don't get crazy! Explain it all.* I took a few deep breaths. "I am separated. I have a seven-year-old son at home. I haven't received child support. I must have this money!" I began to cry.

"Let's see what we can do." He returned from talking to his supervisor and issued me a check for "emergency funds." It was for the amount I would have received. "Thank you more than I can say!" I left knowing that I could be all right for another month.

In court the following weekend, after discussing the fact that I had not received child support, the judge said, "You are so attractive. Why cling to this jerk? I'm sure you can find someone better." This was not what I expected to hear from the court! Crazy talk.

The following day my borrowed car died just as I was about to get on to the Jackie Robinson Parkway to Brooklyn. On the radio, I heard the news commentator say, "There is a red Ford stuck in the right lane."

It was me. I had to laugh. I laughed so hard I cried, but this time I found it really funny—even though the joke was on me! This was crazy!

Post Script: In 2009, the law in NYC changed. If you owed child support, you could not renew your driver's license. You could not get a passport. You could not renew your own working license.

In 2010, I received child support monthly. I thought, he must be alive and fuming. The check comes every second week of the month. And because of interest, I shall be receiving it for a long time to come.

CHAPTER 16

SECOND MARRIAGE
"Complicated Families"

My future husband's uncle called us over to the bar.

"Your father is an asshole," he told Phil. "He should have come to his son's wedding! We love you, Helene. Don't let his and your grandmother's craziness affect you! Enjoy."

Phil and I looked at each other and shrugged our shoulders. We smiled and moved on to the lovely evening that unfolded.

I am Jewish. I am older than Phil. I am divorced and have a son. Phil was brought up Catholic. His father and his grandmother are German. When Phil was born, his dad walked out of the hospital complaining that he wanted a daughter. Phil became the oldest of five children. All of the other four children are girls. When Phil got spinal meningitis in the army and was given the last rites, no one from his family went to Ft. Polk to see him. He came through and was discharged, not having to go to Vietnam as his friends did.

We met when my son was six years old. I was going through a divorce and Phil was so loving and helpful. As a schoolteacher, I was studying for my master's degree. Phil would go with me to help find all the material I needed for my thesis. I worked hard and it was always so much fun together. My son loved Phil. Years later, when my son joined the army and was sent to Iraq, he had to fill out a form (in case he died in action). He said Phil was his father. Phil cried and loved my son even more! When I was introduced to Phil's family at a holiday dinner, Phil said, "This is Helene. She's nine years older than me. She's Jewish. She's divorced. She has a seven-year-old son. We are in love. Let's eat!"

We've remained good friends with one of his sisters, her husband, and daughter. His cousin George was the best man at our wedding and George and his wife remain close. All the rest of the family, even though most of them came to the wedding, have nothing to do with us at all. Several years after we got married, Phil's dad passed away. They had never spoken to each other or interacted in any way since the wedding. Phil's grandmother stuck with her son and had nothing to do with me—the Jewish woman.

I felt bad. I am a good person and would have loved to have a larger family to interact with and share our lives with. I had a brother and have a sister-in-law and parents who loved Phil. I have many, many friends and we all go out together and have fun times.

Phil and I have traveled to France and England, Scotland and Italy. We have gone swimming and played in the waters of many islands around the globe. We have gone to many, many inns and hotels for fun weekends and happy, exciting adventures. We love NYC where we live. We dine at fabulous restaurants and enjoy the theater and everything New York has to offer.

This summer we will be married for twenty-three years. We are happy together through good times and difficult health-related ones. Phil had a defibrillator and pace maker put into his heart, and then ten years later, it was removed! Amazing. Except for his one loving sister, no one visited the hospital. I have had breast cancer and survived. We are lucky!

And our son is now married and has a lovely little five-year-old daughter. It is a thrill to share our lives with them. Families can be complicated; however, life is shorter than we think it will be, and how nice if we can uncomplicate and live with a more open, accepting, loving, caring attitude.

P.S. Many of Phil's sisters' children befriend their uncle Phil on Facebook.

CHAPTER 17

LEARNING TOLERANCE AND UNDERSTANDING

"Teachers, please take a moment to complete this census form. It's a list of your students this year. After each name write the nationality and race of the student."

It was 1975. Black or African American, Spanish, Asian, and Other were listed. I had a problem. I distinctly remembered all thirty-six students' names and personalities. I could not recall their race or nationalities. How could that be? I had known them for one whole month!

I had to wait until the next day when I could look at them and see what was wanted for the census.

My grandfather came from a small town in Russia where people who did not belong to the Tsar's Orthodox Church (Jews) suffered in pogroms. Traditional religious anti-Semitism served as a pretext for pogroms. They were organized locally, sometimes with government and police encouragement. Jews were raped and murdered and their property looted. My grandfather luckily got out of Russia and came to America.

In the early part of the twentieth century, he settled with my grandmother on the Lower East Side of New York City. He was a blacksmith and found a job working with the NYC police department shoeing horses.

"Just remember," Grandpa told his children, "policemen in New York can help you. They are here for you no matter who you are."

When my brother and I were very young, Grandpa would put us on his lap, tell us to touch his nose, and then he would wiggle his big ears until we howled with laughter.

"Grandpa, please tell us a story."

He would tell us stories about his Irish policemen friends. They were always silly and fun and they also showed the humanity of the Irish men on the squad.

People living in the area where my mom was born were Italian, Greek, Irish, and Jewish immigrants, all looking for a better life. They learned to live together and struggled to survive.

My mom first lived on Hester Street. When it was time to paint their apartment, the family did the same thing each time—they moved! This time they found an apartment on Cherry Street. Mom went to Seward Park High School, played at the neighborhood community center, and was part of the tumult of this growing area. She had three sisters and two brothers and a few close friends. My grandma spoke the traditional Yiddish that she came to this country with. Grandpa, my mom, and her siblings all spoke English.

Mom became friends with her next-door neighbor. This gal's brother was Meyer Lansky. Known as the mob's accountant, he was Jewish-American organized crime figure who, along with Lucky Luciano and Bugsy Siegel, made up the Jewish mafia. Mom remembered hearing gunshots fired in the backyard of her ghetto neighborhood, but told us that, otherwise, she had a relatively safe childhood.

"Meyer was so nice to all of us. We really didn't know anything about his daily business. He certainly had a lot of visitors. He always asked if we needed help with anything at all. I'm happy I didn't tell him about anyone I didn't like!"

Mom was introduced to my dad by a mutual friend. Dad was from Brooklyn. His family was quite successful and owned a large store called Meisner's Wallpaper and Paint Store. He drove a Roadster Convertible and often was seen hanging out at theaters waiting to meet chorus girls after the shows. He was rather short and was always looking for the girls at the end of each line.

He had four brothers and one sister. My uncle Al became a doctor, later on removing my tonsils, and my dad was slated to go to dental school. He was brilliant in Boys' High School and graduated with honors. Three of my uncles—Harry, Ben, and George—worked in the store. Dad wanted to work with his brothers and never pursued his further education.

I believe that because Uncle Harry was handicapped, my dad felt he would have more time with him at the store. Harry was born deaf and never really learned to speak. He could read your lips and do everything else. When I was ten or eleven, he liked to comb and style my hair whenever we went to my father's parents. None of the brothers married until they were in their forties, so they were often home with their parents.

My parents eventually married and moved to the Kensington area of Brooklyn where my brother and I were born several years later. My brother was in JHS when I began kindergarten and quite often, many of his friends were around the house. They were fun and liked to tease me, but I didn't care. I loved the attention.

Dad's three brothers worked in the business eighteen hours a day, often sleeping in the store overnight. Dad wanted to work with them but with more manageable hours so he could be with his new family. They said no.

So my dad became his own boss and worked for himself. However, all monies that were to be his from the business were now gone. Dad had Mom and his children and remained working-class poor.

"I'd rather have less money and get to enjoy my life with my wife and children," he said.

On our block, East Second Street, stood a row of six family apartments, each three stories high. Italian, Greek, Irish, and a minority of Jewish people lived there. Across the street were private homes with porches. We loved to play stoop all there, until we were shooed away. PS 230, as well as the subway, was around the corner. The school had many children who attended the local church a half block away. I remember going to the church with my Catholic friends and hoping the Jewish part of God wouldn't be angry with me.

The subway, on the other hand, took us to magical places like Manhattan and Coney Island. Mom only worked when I was in school, so holidays and vacation time were special. We rode the subway into the "Big City." We saw movies, walked through Times Square, went to the top of the Empire State Building, and had lunch in Chinese restaurants and Jewish delicatessens. We took the ferry to the Statue of Liberty and walked through several museums. Coney Island with its beaches and knishes, penny arcades and Nathan's hot dogs, was always delightful.

In our neighborhood, there were Chinese restaurants for chicken chow mein and egg foo yung. Gorelicks was a famous delicatessen for a hot dog or pastrami sandwich. Ebinger's Bakery for blackout cake Also, Scorolla's for pizza. And the Beverly Movie Theater, where on a Saturday afternoon, when most children went to the movies by themselves, if you didn't behave, the matron would flash her lights in your eyes.

Three blocks away was the Flatbush Jewish Center facing Ocean Parkway, a lovely walkway filled with trees and bordering a large boulevard. I loved the horseback-riding lessons I took as a child. We began in Prospect Park and found our way to the paths of Ocean Parkway.

Mom also gave me tap, ballet, and acrobatic lessons, and at age eight, I performed with my class at the Brooklyn Academy of Music, downtown Brooklyn. We were a group of children from several different backgrounds performing for our families and friends. My grandmother was in the audience with a bouquet of flowers for her beloved granddaughter.

Some days we would take the trolley car on Church Avenue and travel to Flatbush Avenue to shop and walk and eat at Garfield's Cafeteria or Jahn's ice cream parlor.

In my neighborhood, my first best friend in the whole world lived on East Second Street next door to my house. His name was and always will be Mr. Stewart. He was the only black man living in this neighborhood.

Mr. Stewart was the janitor of the building next door to ours. He babysat for me, he listened to me. We read books together. He was smart and kind and good and wonderful. He lived with his religious wife who sang glorious gospel songs heard through the walls of the buildings every Sunday morning.

Mr. Stewart also had a job in Manhattan. In the late afternoon, I would wait on the stoop of my building on East Second Street until I saw this dark-skinned man wearing a fedora and clutching a newspaper, coming down the street. I would run to him and say, "Welcome home!" Sometimes he brought me a candy or a little doll. I was so happy to just hold his hand and walk down the street with him.

Neighbors said they were glad that the Stewarts didn't have children. I didn't understand what they meant. Mr. Stewart had me from day one! We would stoke the fire in the basement together. We would laugh and talk and sing. He was always careful and wouldn't let any harm come to me. I felt his genuine warmth and his true, caring spirit. When he passed away, my parents were the only white people in the whole neighborhood who went to the funeral.

My father and mother loved music. They loved to dance in the living room to music on the TV or from the records played on a turntable. They particularly liked Nat King Cole, Louis Armstrong, Frank Sinatra, Dean Martin, and Sammy Davis Jr.

My father was a pretty quiet gentleman. When Nat King Cole was taken off TV because Southern states wouldn't allow a "colored" person on their stations, my father exploded.

"What are they doing? God made us all human beings. It doesn't matter what his color is … He's so talented and we enjoy him! How stupid can people be!"

Before we were born, my parents traveled down South on a trip to a wedding and came across several signs on hotels that said, "Jews and Colored Not Allowed."

When they went to a racetrack, they saw different water fountains and bathrooms for whites and blacks. At that same racetrack, they went upstairs to watch the horses run and were told to leave because only black people were allowed upstairs. When recalling the event, Dad said, "I don't understand the hatred that people have for someone who looks different."

"Remember," Mom repeated several times throughout my childhood, "you can't judge a book by its cover." An avid reader and a caring person, my mom knew what she was talking about and so did we!

CHAPTER 18

TEACHING

The curriculum of the elementary school that I taught in was typical of the 1970–1980 NYC school system. I was at PS 181 in the East Flatbush section of Brooklyn. At the beginning, there were children from many different backgrounds. Several years later, families began to move away from this neighborhood as Haitian immigrants arrived.

All scholastic subjects were taught as well as gym and art. In my fourth grade classroom, I added my own personal subject area. It had to do with tolerance and understanding. "Wow, we are all so lucky to have a classroom with children from so many different backgrounds. Let's share what we know."

We spoke about where our families came from, the different countries our grandparents had come from, and the customs we embraced. Throughout the school, weeks and months leading up to Thanksgiving, we discussed the different holidays each of us celebrated. We talked about kinds of food we ate, clothing we wore, houses of worship, and music we enjoyed at those special times.

We talked about feelings. "How do you think it feels to come into a totally new classroom and not know anyone? What if your skin is a different color than most of the others? What if you don't know the language?"

The children talked and shared and also told of their parents' hesitation with people from different races and nationalities.

I played one of my favorite albums for them. It's from South Pacific and called *You've Got To Be Carefully Taught*:

You've got to be taught to be afraid of people whose eyes are oddly made,
and people whose skin is a different shade,
You've got to be carefully taught.
You've got to be taught before it's too late,
Before you are six or seven or eight,
To hate all the people your relatives hate,
You've got to be carefully taught!

We spent many days talking about the lyrics and what they meant to us. And to those people who prejudge others and those who are the ones who are prejudiced against.

"I don't want to make anyone feel bad," several children said. "I don't want someone to make fun of who I am."

"Let's find out more about other people," I said.

We decide on having an international luncheon a few days before Thanksgiving. All my students' parents and grandparents were invited. Children could wear costumes, bring in objects from their countries, and play music on tape recorders at their seating section. They could all get a chance to taste food from many different countries.

The assignment of the next month: Children had to choose a totally different religion, race, and or country from their own. They had to do research on this new place, create a lovely colorful cover, and share their findings with the class. A separate part of the assignment was to find a simple fiction story about the country they had chosen and read it to all the class.

At our international luncheon, all the staff that were available, as well as teachers on preps or lunch hour, were invited.

This was the beginning of many years of Ms. Oelerich's international luncheon.

Back in the classroom: "Children, how wonderful it would be if a new generation of children, like all of you, could grow up knowing that everyone, no matter where they came from or what color their skin is or what language they speak, everyone has a chance to be special! You can do it. You can't judge a book by its cover! Give everyone a chance."

"Mrs. O, when I get a job someday, I bet all the people in my office will be from different parts of the world. It would be fun to make new friends."

"I think that maybe there wouldn't be a reason for so many wars and fights and things if we try to understand each other."

"Yes," I said. "You're getting the idea!"

"How does it feel if someone makes fun of you? It hurts. Let's treat people like you would like to be treated."

We talked about weight and color and poverty and clothing and all kinds of things that children get picked on for. Everyone agreed to be nice, to try and to talk to their parents about what we learned in school about tolerance and understanding.

I began teaching at PS 209 in Whitestone, Queens, in the 1990s. The population of this school was mainly Chinese, Korean, Greek, Jewish, and Italian. Since this was a school for gifted students, children were bused in from many different areas in Queens. I thought, even little bits of humanity absorbed by my students would go a long way.

The international luncheon came with its talent show and sharing of foods from families who met each other in a warm, friendly classroom and listened to music from far corners of the globe.

I had an idea. Along with the international luncheon, I had Asian students teach the class how to use chopsticks. We excitedly planned a trip to Chinatown, where we all had a delicious Chinese lunch. Parents joined us and it became a yearly tradition. We began in Manhattan's Chinatown and eventually found a lovely restaurant in Flushing to celebrate a new tradition.

I believe that teaching the topics of tolerance and understanding and having fun at the same time was as much a tribute to my family and friends, as it is to my students. I couldn't have felt so completely comfortable with this style of teaching if I hadn't had the background my family and friends afforded me. My way of teaching gave me the opportunity to visualize a better, brighter future for the next generation.

LET YOU BE SOMEONE ELSE

"Hi, David. Welcome to the fourth grade. I'm happy that you're in my class."

David smiled slightly and looked around the room. His parents brought him early to meet me and get his bearings. David was a "select mute." There was no physical reason for him not to speak. His parents told me that they heard him murmur once in a while, but he chose not to talk in school at all. He was a bright young man, did his work, and passed all his tests. He loved to read and I was happy to have him as a student and a challenge.

In my classroom, we had lots of opportunities to share our ideas and feelings. One special event usually occurred in the springtime when I prepared and introduced my students to the world of the theater. Every year my class worked on putting on a show for the entire school. In the past we performed *Guys and Dolls*, *Grease*, and the *Sound of Music*.

What should we do this year? Aha! I knew it. *Little Shop of Horrors*—a tragicomedy rock musical about a hapless florist shop worker who raises a plant that feeds on human blood.

How much fun would that be? I loved the chorus who sang about the events taking place and could be interspersed with different singers.

After a month of reading the script, working on costumes (with parents helping out), putting together scenery and building our plant, Audrey 2—staging, choosing and editing songs, and everything I loved to work on was ready to go. Of course our production had to be scaled down and appropriate for an elementary class production. Songs were finalized; children tried out for parts.

David was interested. I saw a flicker in his eyes. During the tryouts he raised his hand to try for the part of Seymour. "David, you know you'll have to speak in the show and sing too."

"Okay," he said. "I want to do it!" We all looked at him in amazement. He studied. He put on a costume and performed in front of the entire audience. His parents cried and they thanked me a million times. I was thrilled and felt blessed a million times over again. David talked because he could be someone else in a show. He talked forever afterward, and in the following year, he won a prize for the best written poem that he shared with the whole school audience! This is a teacher's prize!

When I taught at PS 181 in Brooklyn, I taught ESL (English as a Second Language) to the children arriving from Haiti. At the beginning, I taught them songs and often they would greet me in the halls by singing "Happy birthday to you." Eventually they learned English and happily said, "Hello. Can't wait to see you!" In March in 1990, I was presented with an award from District 17 as Teacher of the Year.

In summer of 2010, I was contacted by Dianna Martin, a student I taught at PS 181 in the 1980s.

"I'm thrilled to find you on Facebook. Please come to a GTB [Gifted, Talented, and Bright] reunion we're making for you and the other teachers we had."

The party was for us, the teachers who motivated, cared for, and taught our students to feel good about themselves and to reach for the many goals life has to offer.

The basement apartment house in Ft. Greene was set up with ribbons, bows, and delicious food prepared by the party givers. They cried and hugged us and showed us their PHD and master's degrees. They were teachers and lawyers and educated young people. They told us that they became who they are today because of us. It was a very touching, unexpected, and special evening never to be forgotten.

Another incident occurred when I took my students to Chinatown in Manhattan to experience a Chinese luncheon in a "real" Chinese neighborhood. We were walking on Mott Street, and all of a sudden, I noticed that most of my Asian students were trailing behind the class. Several windows displayed Buddhas and each recent arrival from China stopped to bow before each and every Buddha.

CHAPTER 19

PURRRRRRRRRRRRRRRRRRRRRRRRR

Stan. She is a girl … 17 years old. She was named by a first responder
who found her on 9/11. She was named for Afghanistan.

Brian, Phil, and I walked into the North Shore Animal League in Port Washington, New York.

"Sweet-Pea lived until she was seventeen years old and has been gone for a year. It's time to let a new little cat into our lives," said Phil.

I did miss my pet. I remember thinking that adopting Sweet-Pea would be a good distraction for my young son right after I threw his father out of the house. I thought she was a great replacement. The very first cat we saw looked exactly like Sweet-Pea. I began to cry. Phil, Brian, and the attendants escorted me outside.

"I'm sorry. I just felt the loss all over again. Give me a minute and we'll go back inside."

Sweet-Pea, brown with black stripes, smart, loving, and a big part of all our lives was sorely missed. We found a litter of black and white, newly born kittens. Two were sisters and we hold them and love them right away. They were sweet and funny and six weeks old. Brian named the curious one Momo from the *Three*

Stooges—named Mo, Larry, and Curly. I named the shy one Zuzu from Zuzu's petals in the movie *It's a Wonderful Life*.

A few months later, I arrived home from visiting my parents in Florida and found a very warm apartment in need of air. I opened the window. All the rooms in our apartment have screens as well as our terrace, which overlooks the Throg's Neck Bridge. Momo jumped onto the back of the chair behind the desk. She looked out the window and watched the birds fly by. In an instant, she leapt out the window in her desire to catch a bird. We lived on the sixth floor of an apartment building.

"Oh God no!" I screamed. "Help! I can't go and look. Run outside … Oh no!"

Phil had washed the windows while I was away and forgot to pull the screen down. He ran downstairs while Brian and I were panicking, holding each other, afraid to find out what happened. Phil came upstairs with Momo on his shoulder. She went right to her bowl to eat. At the vet's office, she's checked from her tail to her nose and she's purr-fect!

Eight lives left.

Momo was independent and loving, on her own terms. Zuzu was content and watchful as long as she was fed. Two years ago, Momo's allergies got the better of her and she couldn't smell anything. That's when she stopped eating. The doctor said she might not live very long. I asked, Cancer? No! Heart disease? No! "Okay, we'll make her healthy." We gave her medicines. We fed her with a syringe four times a day. We kept her alive. She got stronger and gained weight. She bounced back. Now she was fine. Seven lives left.

Love was restored in our home and Zuzu didn't lose her sister. Momo looked up at me to say thank you. I hugged her and she purred into my soul.

MOMO

Brian named her Momo at only a few weeks old. She was white with brownish/blackish accents on her ears and tail and sweet other parts of her soft, furry body. She was never large and not too tiny. She was the smartest girl. A kitty-cat with an intelligence that was sweet and exact. When I would get ready to bring something outside, she was at the door.

If I began a chore she was interested in, she would be there waiting and anticipating. She was independent and also thoroughly purred into your soul once you held her to your heart. I sang to her, "I love my Momo, my Momo loves me. Don't know no Momo as happy as we. When we're together, we're great company. I love my Momo, my Momo loves me!"

I called her "Mommy's Momo!" When Brian was in Iraq, and we prayed every day for his safe return, I found myself calling Momo Brian. How silly, but how true in the love I felt for both of them.

Momo had a sister. When I chose her from the litter at North Shore Animal League, I decided to get sisters so they would have each other for company.

Momo and Zuzu were together for seventeen years. Now Zuzu is alone and misses her friend. Momo, named for one of the three Stooges, by Brian lived up to her name. *M* for "most fun and missed," *O* for "owned our heart's love over and over again." MoMo "Mommy's Momo!" I will always love her!

CHAPTER 20

THERE WAS A BOY

They moved slowly toward us. We stood in a circle, hugging and crying and smiling through tears. The airport lounge, large and impersonal, disappeared from my view. All I saw and focused on was my son, Brian. He was handsome in his uniform, smiling at us with secrets behind his eyes.

They moved slowly toward us. A man, carrying a broom, shuffled from the left side of the room, walking with a purpose. An older man, with a pronounced limp, came from the right, near the LaGuardia Airport sign beyond the revolving door. A very large gentleman, pushing a cart, moved toward our little group from the rear of the lounge. I felt their presence before I saw them.

"I'm so happy you're home." I held on to Brian and felt the joy spreading through my fast beating heart.

"Yeah, Mom, me too." He hugged me and held me tight. "The trip was awesome too. We got to Germany and switched planes. The plane to New York was first class all the way! The pilot said we deserved it, and wow, it was pretty cool!"

"Excuse me … us," the men said. "We want to talk with you. Welcome home, sir!"

All three men had tears in their eyes. The man with the cart spoke with heartfelt emotion. "When we got back from Vietnam, we were spit on. We were yelled at and told we were no good, told we shouldn't have gone to war! Yeah, it was tough!"

The big guy smiled. "We love you, son. You're a hero. Thank you!"

"Thank you, thank you," a chorus of voices.

"Hey, thank *you*." Brian was clearly amazed. "You are the real heroes!" They said good-bye and slowly walked away.

My son was home and received a warm welcome from me and Phil and from others who cared. I felt so lucky! Fourteen months in Iraq and he was finally home. I silently gave thanks. "Thank you, Lord," I whispered, as we left the airport.

There was a boy, born on October 23, when leaves become a rainbow of colors, when astronauts landed on the moon, a president resigned, and soldiers were returning from the Vietnam War.

He seemed to say, "If you want me, come and get me," and so he was delivered Cesarean style.

There was a little boy who played with GI Joe figures in his bedroom. When his hamster died, he ran for the toy gun he had fashioned out of pieces of wood. "He has to have a twenty-one–gun salute!"

The hamster did, loud and clear, in the ground outside our home.

"Let's play new words again!" Brian clapped his hands. I put words on sheets of colored paper on the floor in his bedroom. "Make a sentence with the words and you win!"

Brian learned to read before he was four years old. As a teacher of many students, I enjoyed these lessons with my own son. I felt that I could enlarge his world by teaching him to scribble and color all over giant pieces of paper and not to ever worry about coloring within the lines.

"Yay! This is so fun. Up, up, and away!"

In school he led all the students in his kindergarten class to the window to watch the first snowflakes of winter fall to the ground. However, at that moment, the teacher was teaching a different subject. She phoned a few times to say Brian's excuses all begin with the words, "But you see ... "

She continued to complain, "Then he tells how, whatever it is, could be done better his way."

There was a young boy who could play Scott Joplin's music by listening to a recording and then finding the notes on our piano. I searched and found The Young People's Concerts at the Orpheus Theater in Lincoln Center. We went every Saturday morning and appreciated the delightful music together. When my friends would visit, they would often say (with a wink) "Goodness, can't he lower that classical music. It's driving us crazy."

When Brian was six years old, I separated from his father. I thought I would be married forever. I knew my husband's weakness for gambling and I wanted to believe him when he said it was no problem and he could handle it. The phone rang.

"Is he there? He better meet me with the money or you'll never see him again!" Mail arrived every day with letters asking for money. The rent had not been paid. My husband arrived home with a new car, a Porsche. The next surprise was a forty-foot boat. The Porsche was replaced by a Cadillac. The boat sunk! I would lie in bed and think, "Where will I be in five years? What will happen to us?"

He cried, "Don't leave me. I'll change, I swear it."

One day when I was teaching, a friend came to tell me she had to speak with me.

"Your husband owes us money. And he's cheating on you!"

I left work with the excuse that I was sick. I drove home in a fog and picked Brian up from the babysitter. My husband was out of town, so I called his secretary. I jumped right in and said, "I hear that my husband is cheating on me." I thought she might say "That's not true!" What she said was "Who told you?"

She also said, "Now I must tell you something that's been on my mind for a long time. You and your son have been driving in a car with no car insurance. He let it lapse a while ago!"

I called him. He was not at the assigned hotel. I found out later that he was at another hotel with his new *Playboy* bunny girlfriend. We separated. I taught in Brooklyn and drove home to Queens every day. One day I left work and couldn't find my car. I thought it was stolen. The police said it had been repossessed and would be sold at auction. My husband used it as collateral to pay off some debts.

Then, my summer paycheck was taken away by the IRS because we had signed joint income tax returns and he didn't pay his taxes. I had to pay because I had a job that could be found. He was self-employed. The courts said he had to pay child support. The checks he sent me were from a bank that had folded.

Brian cried, "I don't care. I want a mom and a dad."

I said, "We both love you and you will see your dad."

He cancelled more than he came. He didn't show up when he was supposed to. He disappointed his son many times. I knew without a doubt that it was good that we separated; however, I felt somewhat responsible for my child's pain.

I was now a single mom, thankfully with a job that allowed me to be home when Brian was out of school.

My mom and dad were very loving and caring parents and grandparents; they recently moved to Florida and were busy with their own lives. We did love visiting them, especially during the cold winter months.

My brother had moved to California, and although he helped me financially with my divorce and listened to my problems on the phone, he was busy building a career for himself in Los Angeles.

Soon after, I began weekly therapy sessions. I found it a huge relief to be able to talk with someone who didn't know me at all. My dreams of smashing my crappy old car into my separated husband's new one were finally expressed.

At the time I got involved in a program called EST (Erhart Seminar Training). This controversial weekend (sixty hours) course allowed participants to achieve a sense of personal transformation and enhanced power. This was extremely helpful in sorting out my life and at a post-session called "Be Here Now," I met Phil.

Phil was honest, smart, flirtatious, and cute. We started to date. Brian wasn't thrilled about me dating anyone and I made sure Phil was not in our home when we would awaken in the morning. After a while, Brian began to enjoy Phil's jokes. We often ate out together, the two of them giggling and having fun.

Phil was nine years younger than me. He was brought up as a Catholic. He was the oldest of five children and the only boy. He had helped raise four sisters. He knew how to treat a gal!

Phil loved to go camping with his cousins.

"Do you think I could go camping with Phil?" said Brian. "I know I'd like it. I could bring my friend Billy and we could wear our army uniforms, and ohh, can I go?"

"Great … He wants to go with me, great. It'll be a blast!" And off they went for a "guys only" camping experience.

Phil had been in the army but illness had prevented him from going to war. He was very patriotic and he often told us about his experiences in Ft. Polk, Louisiana. Brian and Phil played computer games together and laughed hysterically at TV movies like *The Life of Brian* and *Blazing Saddles*. Seeing us together, Brian saw what it was like to have a man love his mother and treat her in a very special way. He began to trust again.

Phil asked me to marry him. I wasn't ready. He said, "I always wanted to have a beautiful wife, I guess I left out 'one of my own.' Now I have someone else's." He said, "When you're ready, let me know. I'm not going away."

I got my divorce. As we left the judge's chambers, my now ex-husband asked, "How come you have a smile on your face?"

I just answered, "Good-bye" and called Phil from the courthouse phone.

"Hey, Phil, just want to let you know, I'm not anybody else's wife anymore!"

At ten years of age, Brian became involved with a senior citizen's group. They were bird watchers. Every year they counted and categorized various birds nesting or passing through New York City. He became their mascot and went with them on Sunday mornings to count birds. They loved having Brian with them. Our bookcases were filled with Audubon information. Around the time of his bar mitzvah, Brian discovered peregrine falcons nesting on the Throgs Neck Bridge right outside our building, in Whitestone, Queens. The bridge could be seen from our living room window. He wrote an article called "A Very Bird's Nest."

"I love all kinds of birds of prey—especially endangered peregrine falcons," he wrote. The entire story was published in *Ranger Rick* on May 1984. The *New York Times* sent a reporter to interview him at our apartment. The next day the interview was reported in the newspaper.

In later years, while in her science classroom at Albany University, my friend's daughter heard a professor talk about a boy and his discovery of falcons in New York. She phoned us and in a very excited voice yelled, "Brian's made history!"

At Brian's bar mitzvah, I was a nervous wreck. I knew we all had to be in the same place together. Fortunately, my family and friends were very supportive and helped me through it all. We danced, we ate, we celebrated and managed to enjoy ourselves. Phil was great. He took all the photos and was extremely friendly to my ex-husband's family. He made it easier for us to all be together.

Unfortunately, many people gave checks and cash as gifts and handed the money to Brian's dad. We never saw one penny of that money! He cashed the checks and disappeared for six years. We thought he might have been in prison. We still don't know for sure.

Brian passed the exam for Bronx Science High School.

"Wow! You're amazing! We're all so excited for you and proud too."

Upon leaving school one day, Brian's father reappeared. After many years of nothing, not even a birthday card, he was waiting outside the school. When Brian got home he said, "Mom, you're not going to believe what happened today! He just showed up and said he'd like to see me sometime. He didn't even say where he'd been. I'd like to see him once in a while!"

"That's okay," I said, an old pain filling up my head. "Just know he may disappoint you again."

"I know but still…"

Brian never wanted to talk about his father. He never expressed any frustration or upset. After several years in therapy, I finally convinced him to have some sessions with my therapist. I brought him to the office and left him at the doctor's door. Before the door was fully closed, I heard the doctor say, "So what's going on with you and your father?" I knew that finally he would have a chance to vent his feelings.

Brian and I had never been apart for any length of time. High school was over and he had been accepted to college in Maryland and was going to leave in September.

"What could I do to ease the way into a separation that wouldn't be too traumatic?"

I decided to work every day at an after-school program to make enough money to send him to Israel for a high school graduation present. While there, he worked on a Kibbutz. He greatly admired and looked up to the soldiers who accompanied and protected his group.

"They walk around with loaded machine guns here. They're awesome. They make everyone feel safe."

I asked Phil if he still wanted to get married.

"Really? Whoo-hoo. Let's do it! We'll have a party and invite all of our friends."

We had a beautiful wedding at the Water's Edge, a restaurant with great food, and a view of Manhattan.

My son and my brother walked me down the aisle. Brian was happy that we were getting married.

"You know, maybe I'll change my name to Oelerich," he said.

Phil's father and grandmother and one brother-in-law did not attend our wedding. They didn't approve of me. They were German and I was Jewish. I was older than Phil and had a child. Phil said, "I'd rather have you in my life than anyone else."

I felt bad because I didn't understand how a parent could not approve of someone who made their son so happy. And I was insulted that they didn't see that I was terrific! Fortunately, the rest of the family came.

There was a boy who studied at the University of Maryland in College Park for one year. He returned home to Queens College so he could enter ROTC program at St. John's University. ROTC stands for Reserve Officers Training Corps. "But of course!" I said to my friends. "From the twenty-one gun salute for his little hamster until now ... no surprise." He also had a new girlfriend in New York and he wanted to see more of her. Eventually, he graduated with a degree in political science.

While in ROTC, he practiced sky diving by jumping out of airplanes. To make extra money, he got a job working for a sport shop in Manhattan and would take groups skiing and snowboarding.

On one trip, he went with friends to Anchorage, Alaska. There he boarded a helicopter, flew over a mountain, jumped out, and snow boarded all the way down! At the bottom he called me.

"Mom, I did it and it was awesome!" Whew! I was so glad he called me at the end not the beginning.

Always the daredevil, although careful, he chose a course in cave diving in his senior year in college. Off to Florida, with yet another girlfriend, Brian's new adventure, diving into the depths of the sea, awarded him certification in night cave diving.

After college, he worked as a civilian for the army at Fort Wadsworth in Staten Island. He was a lieutenant in the army. He was happy and so was I. This was a time of peace after all.

One summer, Brian decided to learn how to play the bass guitar. He played with a band called Nine Lives. He traveled throughout Europe representing his band and when it was called Black Train Jack. The band was sponsored by Sony, and he spent a part of the summer playing in Tokyo and the surrounding provinces of Japan. Brian wrote many songs for the band, one in particular called "Paper Boy." In this song he wrote, "Will my mom be proud of me?"

Yes, I am proud of my son.

On one insane day, the World Trade Center was destroyed by terrorists. Soon after, reservists were called to tour of duty in Iraq. This was the beginning of the Iraqi War.

A giant knot began forming in the pit of my stomach and Phil and I held each other tight.

"Please keep him safe," I prayed.

"Mom, it's not as bad as it looks. I'm part of the civil affairs division of the army. The infantry will go in before us and make sure it's safe when we get there."

"Yes, I'm sure you're right," I said. I wanted him to be right.

Before Brian left Iraq, he had to fill out a form of the army in case he was injured or killed. Phil read the report Brian had filed with the army. Suddenly his eyes filled with tears. Brian had written Phil's name as his biological father.

We agreed to take care of all his banking. This turned out to be a good thing. He was now a captain and training at Ft. Bragg. His team was relocated to a secret area in Europe. From there they would enter Iraq. Unknown to anyone else, we figured out where he was by his ATM withdrawals. We felt like detectives!

Finally, his team arrived in Mosul, at the start of the liberation of this area in Northern Iraq. In the summer, during the months of June and July, his team was sent to the Aqura District, part of the Nineveh Governate.

While there, he helped build schools for women to attend and soccer fields for children to play in. He had a road built to allow villagers to get into the city when there was no way for them and building a school for Kurdish women. It was generally thought that young Iraqi women could not be brought into the twenty-first century. In this school, they learned to use computers and eventually contacted family and friends all over Europe for the first time in their lives.

Written in the *Sun*, a Baltimore, Maryland newspaper, April 21, 2003, was an article about Mosul. It said,

> Captain Brian, who recently arrived in Iraq is in charge of getting the higher-education system functioning. The students felt their lives were finished, said the director of security. There were so few American soldiers, people were surprised to see them, Iraqis gasped and smiled at the small convoy as it hunted for the University of Mosul. What Brian found encouraged him. He was confident that something positive would be done!

This war was different, in many ways, from previous wars. For us there was a way to communicate with our son that helped us get through each day. Every morning in New York City, Brian was getting ready to write his daily report and go to sleep in Iraq. We saw him online and we e-mailed. We could instant message with each other. I know the computer kept me sane. Another day safe!

Once he used Yahoo Messenger to show us where he was and what his barracks looked like. It was amazing to see him sitting in his room, on a hillside in Iraq, while I looked at my computer screen in New York City. Unbelievable!

And then there were the days when we had no contact at all. Those were dark, scary days. Those were the days that you pushed forth positive thinking! We had a Buddha sitting on a table. We made sure that Brian's picture was there. We always had fresh oranges on a dish to honor the Buddha. We also kissed the mezuzah at the front door and stuck a cross that Phil's mom had sent us for Easter into a vase near his picture. Each night we toasted to Brian's good health and safe surroundings before we ate dinner.

No cell phones were allowed on our desks at my school, except mine. It was always sitting on my desk, in case there was a call. No personal communications were allowed at Phil's office. However, his boss placed a red light on his computer that would let him know when Brian was on a line.

We sent letters. We sent candy, pez dispensers, and funny toys. The students and the PTA at my school collected drugstore items like toothpaste and shaving cream. Phil's association at Verizon wanted to support the soldiers in Iraq. They took up a collection to send toiletries and much-needed items to the soldiers, even though they did not work for Phil's company, Sprint. Everything was sent to Any Soldier USA in c/o Captain Brian. He received so many packages that every kid in the village had toothpaste and combs.

Another way to honor Brian and keep myself occupied while he was in Iraq was to trim two large trees with yellow ribbons. All our neighbors helped us decorate the tree in the front of our building. The other tree was in front of the elementary school I taught at. Students helped place the ribbons throughout the tree. They clapped their hands when it was finished. "It looks so great. Can we let him know what we did?" And they wrote letters to Brian and his town. One little girl called me at home about three weeks later.

"Hi, Mrs. Oelerich? It's Katrina. You will not believe it! I got a letter from Brian!"

She read it to me. He thanked her and told her how the soldiers appreciated her concern. He also sent her a special ribbon from the army.

"I can't believe a real-life hero wrote to me!"

At the next assembly day, I thanked all the students for their prayers and for collecting so many useful things for the soldiers and Katrina proudly read her letter from Brian.

He started out as a captain in Mosul, in the civil affairs division, and was promoted to major. He received the Bronze Star for involvement above and beyond the call of duty. He was well thought of by the Kurds in Northern Iraq. He came home safe in body and mind. Fortunately, all his men came home safe too and he didn't have to make any phone calls.

I know he had experiences that would forever change him. He had seen things that he wasn't ready to talk about. He was home and about to begin a whole new life and career and have new relationships that would keep him involved and hopefully happy.

While he was in Iraq, I sent Brian a salami from Katz's delicatessen in Manhattan. Katz's has a famous World War II slogan, "Send a salami to your son in the army" in their window. Not long after he received it, he sent us a picture holding the salami on a hillside in Northern Iraq. I gave the picture to the manager in Katz's. Several months later, I received a phone call from one of Brian's friends.

"You must go on line and find the order section of Katz's deli. There is a picture of your son holding a salami!" Wow ... there was one. And it's still there today.

Post Script

"Mom, come on!"

We walked slowly to the pool. One step at a time. Little feet, little sandals, a tiny hand holding a pail and a shovel. "Mommy, hurry! I want to play in the sand!"

We entered the pool area. Looking back, I can see our apartment building towering over the water's edge.

How beautiful to see the river, the bridge, the sun shining, the birds singing. A lovely summer day, the pool, sand, and kiddy spray, all for us. He's ready for a new adventure! He's three years old. I'm so proud of him.

He walked through the sand. He found it hard to keep his eyes open.

The strong winds blew through the mountains as he walked the hills of Northern Iraq.

The boots we sent him, stronger and more resilient than those issued by the army, helped him get to the enclosed area that was his stronghold. Here he was, a man fighting for our country, making strides that will give him the Bronze Star for bravery above and beyond the call of duty.

In the photo he gave me, women in burkas were sitting behind computers in a school he helped to open, a school that gives women in Iraq a chance to have a better life in the new world to come. They stared up at him as if he is their savior. He is thirty-three. I'm so proud of my son!

CHAPTER 21

TELLING THE TRUTH

Coney Island! The name alone brings back memories of family and friends playing in the sand and splashing in the water, watching fireworks jumping across the summer sky, screaming from the front seat of the cyclone as it makes its way to the top of the world, and Nathan's—the home of the best hot dogs ever!

I recently heard from my junior high school boyfriend Richie Guggenheim. He found me on Facebook and we made a date to meet at Coney Island, in front of Nathan's. When I parked and walked toward Nathan's, the smell of hot dogs and french fries reached out to me. I hadn't been there since the year 2000, when I took my young nephew for his first taste. The time before that was when I graduated from high school and spent the whole night in and around the city, finally reaching Coney Island at five in the morning.

When Richie arrived, it was in a flourish of remembering so many fun things that we did together—going through the Tunnel of Love, walking on the boardwalk, and talking about all the friends we shared our experiences with. Richie went to get us some yummy food while I sat at a small round table under an umbrella.

A young policeman, obviously on a lunch break, was sitting at the next table.

"Excuse me, do you mind if I ask about your tattoo?" he said.

"Of course not. MoMo was my very special cat. I had her for seventeen years, and when she passed away, I put her tattoo on my arm so I could feel her presence every day. She is close to my heart."

"I'm so sorry to hear that she died. My girlfriend just lost her dog and she is very unhappy. I was thinking maybe she would feel better if she had a tattoo of him."

"I have a card from Brooklyn Ink where Alex performed his magic when he worked on me." I gave him the business card.

"Oh, hold on, maybe your husband would mind. Should we wait till he returns?"

"Umm … well, no. Actually my husband is working right now. I'm here with my boyfriend and I know he won't mind!"

I didn't feel like explaining further and I loved the confused "Huh? Oh, umm … okay … what?" remarks from this young man.

"Hehehehe." I giggled too.

He took the photo just as Richie returned and I introduced them to each other.

"Thanks again … 'bye," he said as Richie and I took a little bite out of heaven.

CHAPTER 22

PLEASURE TRAVELING

As I grew up, my desire to travel was fulfilled. On my first trip to Los Angeles, at the age of eighteen, I drove with my parents across the country to meet my brother in Las Vegas. This was an amazing trip through the lovely Pocono Mountains, through hilly Ohio, the outskirts of Chicago, Texas with its oil wells, into unbelievably beautiful Arizona, and finally Las Vegas.

On our travels, I was in charge of where to stay and where to eat. Several times there were young guys in cars that followed us putting signs in their windows. They wanted to know my name and phone number. I thought it was a blast, although my parents were not too happy about this diversion. I stuck a sign in our window, asking, "Where is a good place to eat around here?"

When we arrived in Las Vegas, we stayed at Caesars Palace and reveled in the elegance of this immense hotel, filled with shops and restaurants and tables for gambling. There were no clocks anywhere and people gambled and brought souvenirs and ate at buffets all hours of the day and night. I remember enjoying a magnificent pool area. The weather was extremely hot and dry and swimming in a cool pool was required if you went outside.

I loved playing blackjack and was flattered when a manager asked if I would consider working as a cocktail waitress in the main gambling room. I had just graduated from Erasmus High School and was starting Brooklyn College in the fall.

"Hey, Mom, Dad … what do you think about me taking a job here for a while?"

"You are too cute," Dad said. "Let's eat!" That was his way of ending the conversation.

After Vegas, we drove to Los Angeles and spent a week visiting the beach, the MGM studios, Disney World, and a variety of restaurants and hang-outs that my brother knew. I loved being with him, although I found his world so different from ours and I felt a bit lost and disconnected from "my hero."

We talked about school and friends and boyfriends and music and lots of things. We didn't talk about how much it pained me for him to be so far away from us. He promised to continue visiting whenever he had a chance and that proved to be quite often, thank goodness.

Our drive home from Los Angeles to New York was exhausting and miraculous at the same time. We had early breakfasts in diners with cowboys who ordered steaks and many cups of coffee before their days' work began. We looked up at magnificent mountain ranges and cherished the unusual flowers that grew in the desert.

When we arrived in New York City, my dad only wanted to go to Katz's Deli on Houston Street for a Jewish lunch of pastrami on rye with coleslaw and a root beer. After lunch, Mom and Dad sighed, "Now we are home!"

My travel dreams had started. In the future, I would travel to China with teachers and principals from my school district. Shanghai, Suzhou, Nanjing, and Beijing were rich with history and appealing in all ways. My twenty-two days with educators in China were spectacular.

My travel dreams have come true. I have traveled to Paris five times. Provence is one of my special memories. I love Switzerland (St. Moritz) and Italy (Florence and Rome and Venice). I've traveled to England and Scotland, Prague, and all over Canada.

My life has been filled with cherished stories of my travels to New Mexico (Albuquerque, Santa Fe, Taos) and Colorado. My travels to Washington's Seattle and Vancouver and Victoria Island fill me with the natural beauty and riveting stories of these regions.

So many stories that are now my stories, my experiences, and not just those I have read about. Now I look forward to reading, writing, traveling, and enjoying having all my dreams coming true.

EDUCATORS TRAVELING TO CHINA

"Take me out to the ball game,
Take me out to the crowd.
Buy me some peanuts and cracker jacks.
I don't care if we never get back…"

The couples on the floor dance dramatically around the room. Heads dipped, elbows rose above smiling faces. The CD ended and an excited group of beautifully dressed men and women began singing and dancing to the next song.

"Edelweiss, Edelweiss,
Every morning you greet me.
Small and white, clean and bright
You look so happy to meet me
Blossom of snow may you bloom and grow,
Bloom and grow forever.
Edelweiss, Edelweiss bless my homeland forever."

Singing in perfect English, the *Sound of Music* was never sung with more sincerity. Both songs sounded right out of a recording studio. "Huh? What?" Then laughter and disbelief!

The previous week I had landed in Shanghai, China, with a group of educators from New York City. It was 100 percent humidity and 105 degrees. Exhausted and exhilarated to be in this amazing country, we passed out in our hotel room.

That week was quite interesting as Shanghai, in 1999, was a conglomeration of bikers carrying baskets of fish held by a long bar across their shoulders, as well as BMWs filled with businessmen in dark suits going to brand-new hotels for conferences.

Men wore what Americans would call pajamas in the streets and were given haircuts on the sidewalks. Beggars broke their children's arms and legs to illicit sympathy and get money from tourists.

The skyline resembled a wacky cartoon—high-rise buildings, skyscrapers, and *hutongs* (areas of very poor people coping to survive). Restaurants serving delicious pork, shrimp and duck dumplings also offered turtles, snakes, and things I didn't want to know about. "Oh my God, they brought us a whole turtle—shell, head and tail!" Our guide asked the server to please forgive the Americans and bring something else. Eek! They brought it back, only this time they cut it up checkerboard style." Oyyy!

There was amazing art work at the Shanghai Museum, wonderful walks at the Bund, an embankment on the waterfront that resembles the Seine in Paris, as well as karaoke evening.

After one week, we traveled to an area several miles away on the Huangpu Shanghai River. The entire landscape looked like the photos and drawing I'd seen in books about China from hundreds of years ago; Sampans with fishermen, coolies in triangular hats bending low in rice fields and waving to our welcoming hands. We were to spend five days at a hotel in a remote area learning the language, history, and Tai Chi.

In the evening, we were at the hotel dancing and singing. "Take me out to the ballgame" and "Edelweiss" just cracked us all up; however, we were polite and covered our mouths so as not to insult our new friends!

We joined in with the singing and laughing and trying out our new learned language creating an awesome experience in an amazing country.

LOST

LOST in a myriad of beautiful thoughts.

LOST in amazing adventures here and abroad.

LOST in a world of fascinating books.

LOST during sexually, intimate lovemaking.

LOST sensually dining in incredibly romantic restaurants.

LOST engrossed in exciting movies.

LOST experiencing beguiling sunsets.

LOST watching my plants thrive and grow.

LOST to the beauty of riding a horse-drawn sleigh in New Hampshire, covered in fur wraps and drinking champagne.

LOST in a poem, pulled on a dog sled through a park in Vermont while snow softly floats above and around my heart.

LOST in the magnificence of nature, walking through autumn leaves.

LOST at thrilling theatrical performances, musical extravagances, incredible dance spectacles.

LOST in our warm, cozy room on a winter day, reading a story to my child as the sunlight streams in through the blinds.

LOST in the moment.

LOST in the happiness of life.

LOST in a myriad of sadness and fear.

LOST when my father died, losing my way through the funeral with a fever of sadness.

LOST when my mother slipped away, her dementia staying with me for two years as I found my way without her.

LOST in the *loss* of my brother even as I write these words.

LOST discovering my ex-husband's deception—divorcing him with a smile.

LOSING my mind with my son in Iraq ... not hearing from him—until I did!

LOST when my pets died—heartbreaking pain of losing their gifts of love.

LOST and scared from my losses—unprepared and emotionally drained from life's harshness.

LOST in the intricate fabric of *life*.
Excited for the sunrise
Looking for flowers to grow
Phones to ring, friends to play
Classes to start, restaurants to dine in
Bookstores, libraries, museums to open
Shopping to start, cats to meow
Music to play, cars to travel
A husband to love with, a home to grow in
LOST in the *amazing diversity* of my life.
A Leo, I look for the sun to shine on me.
Every day I say, "Thank you, Lord, for this beautiful day."
LOST and ALIVE in the next experience and adventure.

More Traveling

Under the EL it was dark, murky, and scary. Shadowy figures of men, bundled in shades of gray, moved without purpose, stumbling along, their heads bent from the unrelenting wind. Noise from trains above shattered the silence of a winter day. Long shadows were cast from iron cars. Smoke and sparks reached the ground as the trains sped by.

I was about sixteen years old, going home to Brooklyn after eating lunch at Katz's Delicatessen on Houston Street in Manhattan. My family and I were passing through the Bowery, famous for its flop houses overflowing with homeless, sick, and alcoholic-dependent men. They frightened me. Mom said, "Once upon a time they were babies who had mothers. What a shame to wind up alone and sick."

I remember looking up and seeing a balloon flying into the clear, bright winter sky. I felt a surge of hope. I kept my eyes on the balloon so I could not see those people wandering around and lying in the street. I thought, *I'm not afraid now.* I watched the balloon dancing around the clouds. It seemed clean and fresh and safe up there. Up there a mother will keep her children safe from harm.

I believe the seeds of traveling were planted in me that day. And I continue to soar to new places in my travels around the world. I love to travel. I recall visiting relatives in Toronto as a child, traveling in a sleeping car speeding through the night. I remember rowing on Lake George with my teenage brother, searching for driftwood so he could carve out a lamp for his room.

My first trip abroad was to Paris. We saw the Seine from a circled window inside the Musee D'orsay, dined in Jules Verne in the Eiffel Tower, viewed Notre-Dame from the windows of Tour d'Argent, and celebrated our July 14 anniversary on the Batteau-Mouche, as orchestras on either side of the river played "I Love Paris" and fireworks danced in the sky. I watched the artists in Montmartre and lit candles in Sacre-Coeur. I walked through the Luxembourg Gardens and the Louvre. I ate and drank and loved in romantic Paris.

And then there's Italy—Venice and Florence and Rome. Tartufo in the Piazza Navona at Tre Scalini, lunch outside a church in Trastevere, Rome. Breakfast on the Tounibouni Beachi rooftop in Florence, and a dog jumps in the fountain in the Piazza Signorina on a blistering hot summer day. Venice, so full of wonder, boating in Vaporettos, pausing under Marco Polo's home.

St. Moritz, where it snowed in August and the postal bus rode us down to Castanola in Southern Switzerland. Swans in the Limmat in Zurich where birds ate from our break basket and we had to pay for each slice while the trolleys passed by.

London's Drury Lane Theatre, even more exciting than the *Miss Saigon* show. And Scotland's quiet streams where we could sit and picnic surrounded by hundreds of sheep.

Driving across America through the hills of Ohio, the mountains of Utah, thrilled by wild blooming cactus in Nevada, gambling in Las Vegas, the mountains and fog surrounding California, and horseback riding in the foothills of Palm Springs.

And my honeymoon in San Francisco, returning several times to relive the pleasures of that city: Chinatown, cable cars, the Golden Gate Bridge, and giant redwoods looking majestic and evoking religion as the sun filtered through the Muir woods.

Southern California's Los Angeles, the San Diego Zoo, and drinking coffee on a street in La Jolla lined with lemon trees.

A long Columbus weekend playing hooky from work, in the magical city of Prague.

The island of Aruba with her divi-divi trees, St. Martin, St. Thomas, Puerto Rico, and the fun-filled days and nights in Cancun swimming with dolphins and skimming the water in speed boats on the way to the coral reef.

Arriving in China after twenty-two hours of flight—Shanghai, Beijing, the Great Wall, the Opera, and the hutongs of olden times, mixed with strange new structures emerging as part of the new China skyline.

Santa Fe and Taos, hummingbirds at the Rio Grande, Native Americans dancing at their pow-wow. Southern Colorado with its whispering sands in the Sangre de Christo Mountains.

New Orleans drenched with music and amazing food, celebrating life at the jazz fest.

Throwing snowballs in the summer at Rocky Mountains Glacier National Park, rafting in Flathead Lake, Montana, while eagles soar above.

Seattle and the Bouchart Gardens of Victoria Island. Vancouver with its lochs and the salmon returning to their home.

New England, Vermont: Woodstock's Village Green, border collies rounding up Asian ducks in Killington Mountain. Dog sledding in Northern Vermont through a space in the snow, a horse-drawn sleigh in New Hampshire, a warm blanket and a bottle of champagne.

And New York's Montauk, Long Island. A place for long walks on the beach, relaxing evenings and fun.

My waterfront home allows me to fly with the seagulls, listen to the waves, and hear the geese as they take flight. They are my balloons seen from my windows.

They bring me comfort, exhilaration, and dreams of the next adventure.

What I See Out My Window Every Day

MoMo

Stan

ZuZu

Zuzu jumped into Phil's arms in bed (never did that before) and would not leave his side when he was 49. Went to doctor and he had a heart condition. Zuzu saved his life!

MoMo & ZuZu have passed but were with me for many years. I have a tattoo of MoMo on my arm.

120

Helene Meisner Oelerich

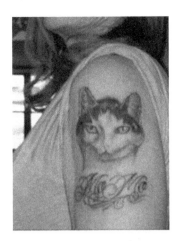

Erasmus Hall High School

About the Author

Helene Meisner Oelerich is a writer, teacher, photographer, reviewer of restaurants, traveler, and loves to read.

Known as "Dining Diva," she writes reviews for magazines and newspapers.

She is a mom, wife, and friend. She loves her cat, Stan, a female cat found on 9/11 and named Stan for Afghanistan.

She holds a BA from Brooklyn College, an MA from Queens College, plus fifty credits toward a PHD.

She loves dining out in spectacular New York City and enjoying theater and everything Manhattan has to offer.

She lived in the Kensington area of Brooklyn most of her life and now resides in Beechurst, Queens.